# PENJING

## The Chinese Art Of Miniature Gardens

Article by Hu Yunhua
Photographs by Deng Yongqing and Jin Baoyuan
Illustrations by Wang Zhiying
Edited in Chinese by Zheng Guanghua

TIMBER PRESS
*1982*
*in cooperation with*
*THE AMERICAN HORTICULTURAL SOCIETY*

TIMBER PRESS
P.O. BOX 1631
Beaverton, Oregon 97075

Library of Congress Cataloging in Publication Data

Hu, Yunhua, 1943-
  Chinese miniature plants.

  1. Gardens, Miniature. 2. Bonsai. 3. Gardens, Chinese.
I. Deng, Yongqing. II. Jin, Baoyuan. III. Wang, Chih-
ying. IV. Title. V. Title: Penjing, China's bonsai art.
SB433.5.H78      635.9'772      82-823
ISBN 0-917304-70-5          AACR2

# CONTENTS

# I. A General Introduction

Penjing, the Chinese art of miniature gardens created with trees or rocks, had its origins long ago in Chinese history. In 1972 Chinese archaeologists unearthed an ancient tomb in Shaanxi Province. Built in 706 A.D., it contained the remains of Prince Zhang Huai, second son of Empress Wu Zetian of the Tang Dynasty. The murals on the walls of the tomb depict court life. Two of these, to the surprise of horticulturalists, show ladies-in-waiting, in court attire, holding potted landscapes with miniature rockeries and fruit trees (fig. 1). These are probably the world's earliest pictorial records of penjing, showing that this art form was appreciated in the imperial court more than 1,200 years ago. Throughout the ages penjing has acquired a distinctive national character and a unique style in the hands of master craftsmen and connoisseurs. Its beauty is that of a ''solid painting'' or a ''silent poem''.

Penjing is an art which recaptures nature in a concentrated way, using stones and trees as raw materials. It differs from the potted plant in that the latter is simply grown for appreciation. In penjing the trees and stones are treated artistically as part of an integrated natural scene.

''A range of mountains stretching a hundred *li* in a little tray'' — with a few stones and trees the miniature landscapist is able to recreate the complexity of nature through his art, refining, summarizing and enhancing nature while giving expression to his own concepts and feelings. Penjing charms with its poetry and imagery, achieving an effect which stems from but surpasses nature.

Penjing falls into two main categories: Miniature trees and miniature landscapes. The trees used for the first usually have gnarled old roots and trunks that have been trained into shape over many years. This form of penjing is most commonly known by

Fig. 1

its Japanese name "Bonsai", and it can be classified by tree type such as pines and cypresses, the various other kinds of trees and the fruit trees. In the miniature landscapes stones are the main components, supplemented by grass, moss, boats, bridges and pavilions — a miniaturization of mountains and rivers. These landscapes may be further subdivided into dry landscapes, with the tray filled entirely with earth (fig. 2), water landscapes, with the tray filled with water (fig. 3), and the dry-and-water type, (fig. 4) with the tray containing both water and earth. A landscape with a suggestion of water is sometimes created by filling the tray with earth and sprinkling a few pebbles on top to represent water.

Trees used in Penjing have a great diversity of shapes. They may resemble weather-beaten veterans in the wilderness, or tower aloft with spreading canopies. They may hang down from precipices like dragons spreading their claws, or look gnarled and knotted. Some have drooping branches, others have flowers and fruits hanging on boughs. Furthermore, miniature landscapes are living objects of art which change according to the season of the year. In spring crabapple (*Malus spectabilis*) blossom bursts forth, flowers hang on the wisteria (*Wisteria*) vines like strings of bells, azaleas (*Rhododendron simsii*) blaze in a riot of colour, Chinese peashrubs (*Caragana sinica*) blossom like spreading wings and elms put forth green buds. In summer wisteria casts a dense shade. In summer the ginkgo (*Ginkgo biloba*) and hedge sageretia (*Sageretia theezans*) are covered with gold, while the fruits of nandina (*Nandina domestica*), pomegranate (*Panica granatum*), firethorn (*Pyracantha*) and Chinese wolfberry (*Lycium chinense*) hang heavy on the boughs. In winter the sloping branches sway in the wind while the wintersweet (*Chimonanthus speciosa*) and pine

Fig. 2

Fan-shaped marble sheet glued with axinite planted with *Pseudolarix kaempferi*. Height of marble sheet: 25 cm.

Hedge sageretia growing as if on a withered trunk. Height: 56 cm.

Fig. 3

Fig. 4

appear even more vigorous in the ice and snow. Many of the trees in miniature gardens have been cultivated, with painstaking care, for tens or even hundreds of years by generation after generation of experts.

A miniature landscape may represent a solitary peak or a chain of mountains. The views can be so varied that one can appreciate the ever-changing landscape without having to go outdoors.

Tree penjing can be classified according to height as large (80-150 cm), medium (40-80 cm) or small (10-40 cm). Those exceeding 150 cm are exceptionally large while those under 10 cm are minute. (Note: The height of a tree penjing is measured from the surface of the tray to the crown of the tree, and in the case of the overhanging type the length from the base of the trunk to the crown of the tree is used. The length of a miniature landscape is measured by the length of the tray.) A miniature penjing may be held in the palm of the hand and, despite its tiny size, it still retains the beauty of the wilderness. By their special method of cultivation, penjing artists are able to stunt the growth of finger-size trees which will look little changed in size or shape after dozens of years, yet still regenerate flowers and leaves from year to year.

Penjing add charm to a park and give a sense of space when placed around a room, bringing a sense of relaxation and contentment. Creating and enjoying one's own penjing helps shape one's temperament and enhances one's artistic accomplishments. That is why in the past penjing was both prized in the imperial court and widely popular among the common people. They served as major objects of beauty on display in parks, restaurants, public buildings and homes, and definite records of this role can be found in the histories of past dynasties.

A painting by the Tang Dynasty court painter

Fig. 5 — (1) shows a tree before pruning.

Yan Liben (?-673 A.D.), for example, shows, among those paying tribute to the court, a man holding a tray with an exquisitely formed miniature landscape bearing a remarkable resemblance to its modern counterparts. Han Yu and Du Fu, eminent Tang poets, wrote verses in praise of penjing. During the Song Dynasty (960-1279), countless poems and paintings mentioned or recorded them, such as the works of Zhao Zigu and Du Wan. The Ming (1368-1644) and Qing (1644-1911) Dynasties saw a further popularization of this art and many writers devoted pages in their works to the description of penjing. Ceng Mianzi, for example, said in his *Records of the Customs of Wu:* "The rich build gardens by digging ponds and making hills while the poorer off manage to amuse themselves by creating miniature gardens and landscapes."

The art of penjing spread far and wide throughout the vast area of China. Because of the different varieties of trees used, the techniques employed in their creation and the artists' differing interests and accomplishments, a great diversity of styles emerged which gradually led to the formation of distinctive local schools. Among the better known areas producing penjing are Suzhou and Yangzhou in Jiangsu, Guangzhou in Guangdong, Chengdu in Sichuan, Xixian County in Enhui and Shanghai.

Suzhou penjing feature elm, hedge sageretia and pomegranate, with antique looking trunks and round, tender green leaves. They are famed for their graceful and antique appearance. Guangzhou horticulturalists, who are also known as the Lingnan school (south of the mountains), use elm, hedge sageretia, jasmineorange (*Murraya paniculata*) and Fujian tea bush (*Carmona microphylla*). Their style is elegant and natural, with a touch of the wild. The Yangzhou school coaxes the trunks of pine, cypress, elm and box (*Buxus sinica*) into the

Fig. 5 — (2) shows a tree after pruning.

Fig. 5 — (3) shows a tree after it has acquired a fixed form.

shape of writhing dragons. The leaves look like floating clouds and small inch-long twigs are twisted into triple coils. Chengdu penjing artists mainly employ yew podocarpus (*Podocarpus macrophylla*), *Serissa foetida* and flowering quince (*Chaenomeles lagenaria*), with thick, old trunks looking magnificently dignified. The Xixian County gardeners train the trunks of cypresses and plum trees (*Prunus mume*) to curl upward like dragons. Because Shanghai was the hub of land and water communications, penjing from many places came there, even from as far away as Japan. The Shanghai craftsmen have, therefore, absorbed the techniques of others and created a distinctive style of their own. They use a wide variety of trees but the species preferred are pine and cypress. Crooked or straight, they look natural, ancient and picturesque.

The history of Shanghai penjing can be traced back to the reign of Longqing and Wanli of the Ming Dynasty (1567-1620). It is recorded that Zhu Xiaosong, a bamboo carver, was adept at shaping small trees for connoisseurs of penjing. In the past, however, most penjing were created for the rich and powerful who enjoyed them in their secluded yards and elegant studies. Tasteful works were seldom displayed in parks, nurseries or public places. After liberation in 1949, in order to promote this art and enrich people's lives, the Shanghai gardening departments opened areas in parks and nurseries to support the creation of penjing. Amateur penjing landscapists in the city have set up a penjing association for the swapping of expertise and display of finished products to popularize and promote their art.

The Longhua Penjing Garden in the Shanghai Botanical Garden is the largest penjing centre in the city. It has in its collection outstanding works from

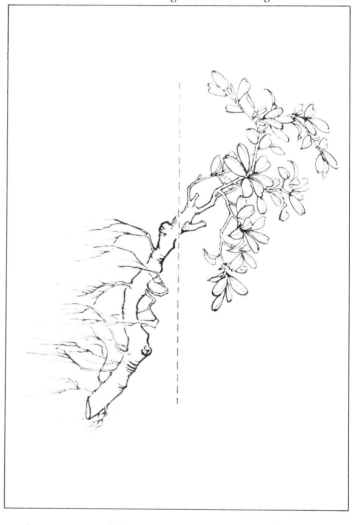

Fig. 6 shows a cutting from a box tree.

various parts of the country as well as thousands of its own creations. Its experienced craftsmen are doing research into the art of producing miniature gardens and landscapes. In recent years, Shanghai penjing have been shown in exhibitions held in Canada and West Germany, gaining a number of awards. Shanghai penjing are now sold in many countries in the world, and appreciated by many foreign friends.

# II. Tree Penjing

Fig. 7 shows the root of elm being coiled up.

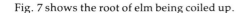

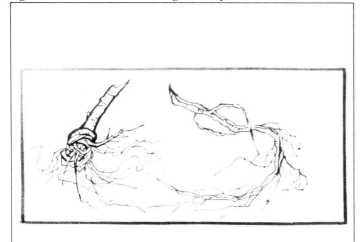

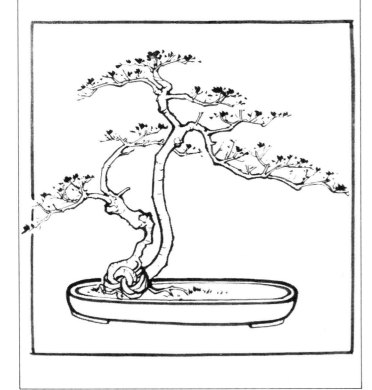

Fig. 8  A penjing made by the method shown in Fig. 7.

## (A) SELECTION OF TREES

In China there are numerous species, about 160 in all, suited for miniature gardens. Generally those preferred are long-lived, have slender branches, tiny leaves, vigorous growth and a high survival rate after transplantation, and lend themselves to pruning. Trees with bizarre trunks and roots, and gorgeous flowers and fruits are the most sought after. They are either found in the wild or propagated artificially.

*1. Natural trees.*

(1) Type of tree: Stunted trees can often be found by the side of streams, roads, bridges or in rock crevices. Many are stunted by years of repeated cutting back and the growth left often appears antiquated and strange. After they are dug up, trimmed and shaped they serve as ideal material for miniature gardens.

Species that are generally obtainable include: elm, hedge sageretia, nandina, cape jasmine (*Gardenia augusta*), Chinese peashrub, trident maple (*Acer buergerianum*), Chinese holly (*Ilex cornuta*), bamboos, wisteria, *Loroptalum chinense*, firethorn, *Sabina chinensis*, *Evonymus bungeana*, nengundo chastetree (*Vitex negundo*), hawthorn, *Serissa foetida*, *Evonymus fortunei*, Japanese holly (*Ilex crenata*), thorny elaeagnus (*Elaeagnus lpungeana*), Chinese wolfberry, box, silverleaf cotoneaster (*Cotoneaster pannosa*), *Eurya emarginata*, Japanese ardisia (*Ardisia Japonica*), *Damnacanthus indicus*, etc.

(2) Time of collection: Select and note the location of the required trees in autumn before they become dormant. Most deciduous types and conifers are ready for digging after they become dormant, but those less resistant to cold will have to wait until the temperature becomes milder so as to save them from frost damage. Trees like these may

Fig. 9

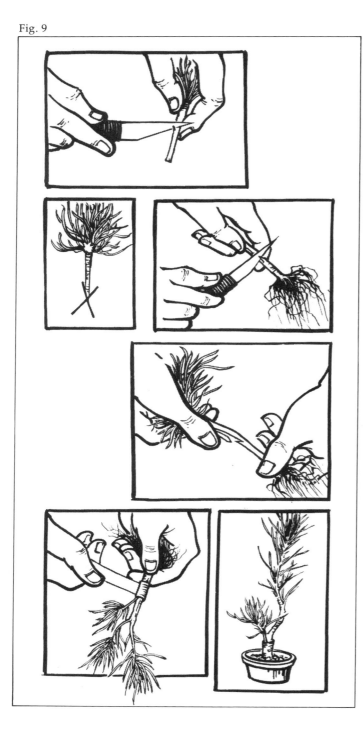

also be removed in the rainy season.

(3) Method of digging: Take along pickaxes, handsaws, shears and baskets. Select those stunted trees that are stout and graceful. Remove most of the branches according to the shape desired, leaving only the trunk and some of the main branches. Dig up the stump with a pickaxe, being careful to preserve as many branch roots and rootlets as possible. Sever the taproot with a smooth clean cut to facilitate healing. After dipping the roots in mud to prevent their drying out, the stumps should be put into a basket which is packed with moss to keep them moist during transportation. Evergreens with less vigorous growing power such as pines, cypresses and Chinese box should not be stripped of all leaves or they will not grow. On the other hand, vigorous species such as cape jasmine, hedge sageretia and nandina will survive even if stripped of all leaves and branches.

(4) Cultivation: The trees need a second pruning when they arrive in the work room. (Fig. 5-1 shows a tree before pruning, fig. 5-2 shows a tree after pruning and fig. 5-3 shows the tree after it has acquired a fixed form.) The length of the roots and branches to be left after cutting is determined by the shape of the tree and the dimensions of the pot. The tree is then planted in an earthen pot or in the nursery bed. The first watering should be thorough and the trunk should be covered with straw or moss. Those with tall trunks should be wrapped with moss to reduce the evaporation of moisture. As the weather gets warmer they should be sprayed with water every morning and evening so that the covering remains moist while the soil is not too wet. Trees with a low resistance to cold should be put in the hothouse over the winter.

After they begin sprouting the covering should gradually be removed from the trees or the buds

Fig. 10

Fig. 11

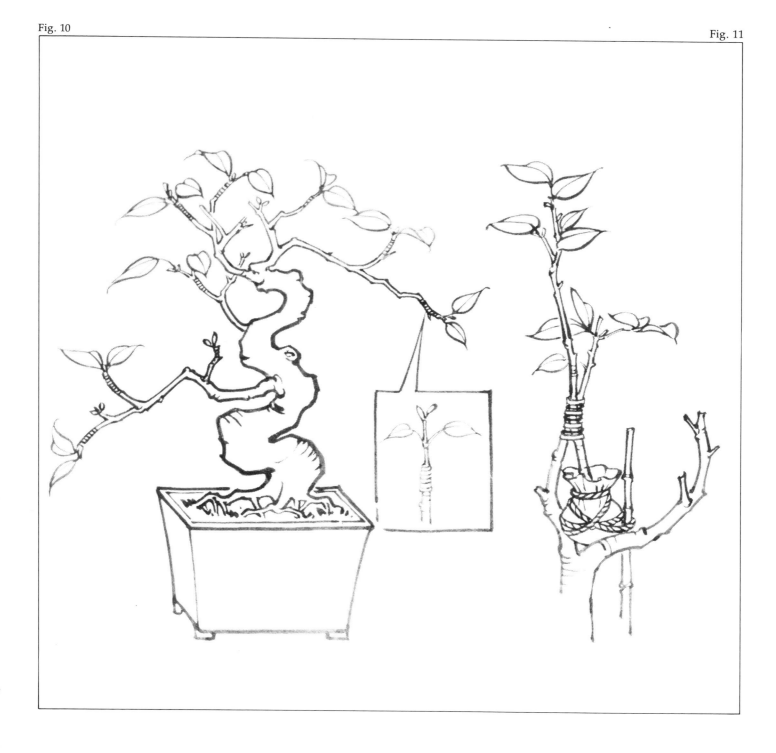

Fig. 12

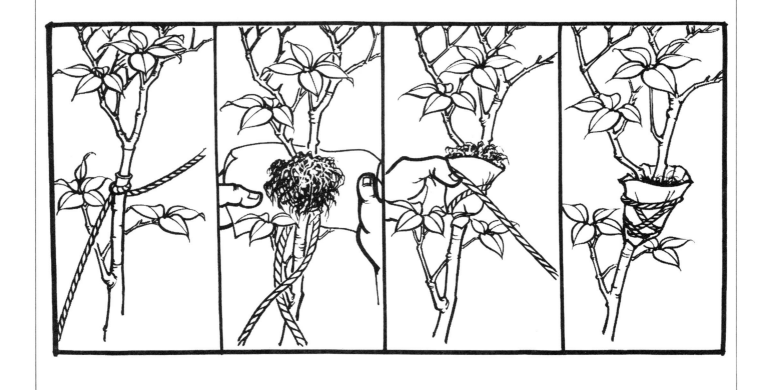

Fig. 13

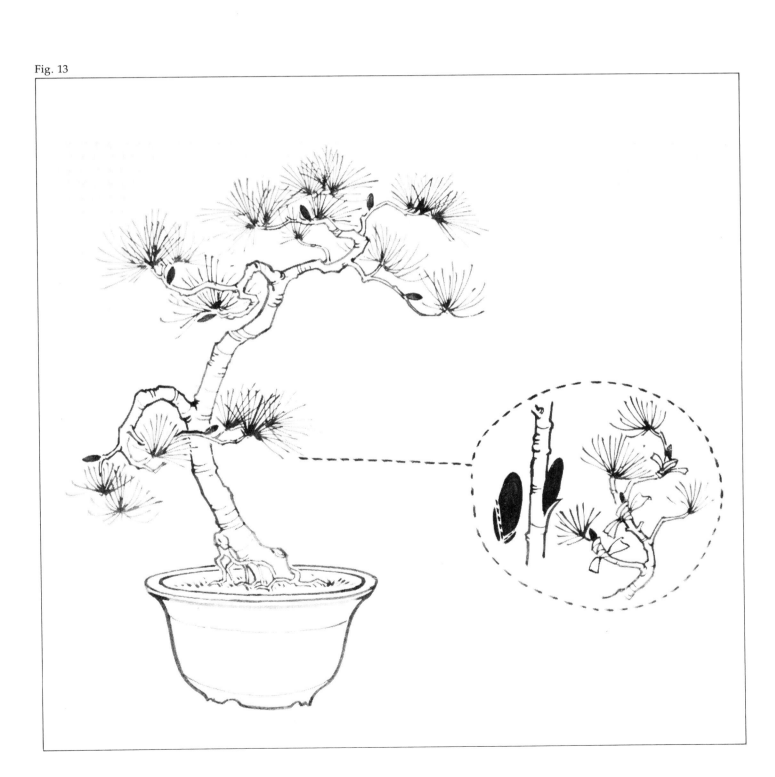

will grow tall and slender and turn yellowish. They should be placed under cover to prevent the buds being scorched by the sun and to reduce evaporation of moisture from the leaves. After a month, gradually cut down the time spent under shade. When the buds are 5 cm long, pick off those poorly located and apply a small quantity of fertilizer to boost the growth of branches.

When the young branches of elm, hedge sageretia and Chinese wolfberry become semi-woody, pick off the leaves and bind the branches with wires to train them into shape. Apply a small quantity of fertilizer to stimulate the growth of new branches and leaves. Prune regularly until the branches form tiers one above the other.

*2. Artificial propagation.*

Some trees for miniature gardens cannot be obtained in the open country and must therefore be propagated artificially. The methods adopted include seeding, cutting, grafting, layering and air layering. Seeding and air layering techniques are similar to those employed generally for growing plants for parks. The following description therefore concentrates on methods used specifically for propagation of plants for miniature gardens.

(1) Cutting.

(a) Cuttings from the branches of older tree: This method is used especially for mature branches which are already graceful in appearance. Once they are established, with a little shaping they make excellent miniature gardens, saving a lot of time. A box, for example, will take some ten years to grow from a seed to a finger-size tree, whereas a branch of the same size propagated by cutting may be used in a miniature garden the same year. Experiments with branches of 1-2 cm diameter or thicker from box, wisteria, elm, hedge sageretia, cape jasmine, Chinese holly and star jasmine (*Trachelospermum jaminoides*) have been successful.

The procedure is as follows: Cut off a well-shaped branch, keeping a few leaves in the case of an evergreen. Place it in sand with only the tip exposed. It will root in a couple of months. This method can be used any time during the growing period, but the cuttings should be screened when the mean temperature exceeds 20°C. Alternatively, if they are not screened they should be sprayed with water regularly to keep the leaves moist. Cuttings propagated in this way benefit from the sunlight, have a high survival rate and will root quickly. Even red maple which does not root easily will do so in about 35 days by spraying. Branches treated with methy-naphtyl acetate and other growth promoting agents will root even more readily. (Fig. 6 shows a cutting from a box tree.)

(b) Cutting from roots: Roots can often be obtained when a pot is emptied or from stunted trees in the countryside. Taproots of wisteria, flowering quince and Chinese peashrub can all be used in this way and will make very good material for miniature gardens. Long roots need not be trimmed but should be wound up. (Fig. 7 shows the root of elm being coiled up and fig. 8 shows a penjing made of elm roots.) Root cuttings will develop buds at their tip. If the growth of buds is desired elsewhere, scratch the bark of the root at the appropriate points and buds will grow from them.

(2) Grafting: This method is applied where cutting is not easily successful. It is also used for those species which do not produce seeds or vary greatly when propagated by seeding.

Grafting can be performed in a number of ways. The following are the most common for the propagation of trees for miniature gardens.

(a) Cleft grafting into the side of the tree: Trees

Fig. 14 — (1) Straight trunk.

Fig. 14 — (2) Leaning trunk.

Fig. 14 — (3) Double trunk.

Fig. 14 — (4) Recumbent trunk.

Hedge sageretia, withered trunk. Height: 57 cm.

*Serissa foetida*, straight trunk. Height: 50 cm.

Yew podocarpus, straight trunk. height: 45 cm. Most of the roots are
exposed.

Chinese holly (*Ilex cornuta*), double trunk, with tiny leaves. Height: 59 cm.

*Artemisia abinthium*, slanting trunk, with fragrant leaves. Height: 78 cm.

Chinese holly, double trunk. Height: 26 cm. Otherwise known as "no bird perches" because of its thorns, it bears crimson fruits in autumn.

Cape jasmine (*Gardenia jasminoides*), slanting trunk. Height: 30 cm.
This puts forth white, intensely fragrant flowers in summer and bears
orange-coloured fruits in autumn.

Chinese elm, slanting trunk. Height: 20 cm. This was propagated by root cutting and has been growing for 26 years. If planted in earth, it may attain over 20 m.

Fig. 14 — (5) Overhanging trunk.

Fig. 14 — (6) Semi-overhanging.

Fig. 14 — (7) Crooked trunk.

Fig. 14 — (8) Multiple trunk type.

Fig. 14 — (9) Grove type.

Fig. 14 — (10) With stone.

Fig. 14 — (11) Withered trunk.

Fig. 14 — (12) Connected root.

cultivated by this method have no clearly visible graft joints and are therefore more beautiful. The stock can be re-used when a first attempt fails. The best time for cleft grafting is one month prior to the budding of the tree. For Japanese white pine (*Pinus parviflora*) and *Pinus aspera*, for example, select a 2-3 years old healthy Japanese black pine (*Pinus thunbergii*) sapling as stock. Cut off part of its branches and leaves. A scion, 10 cm long with 6 to 8 tufts of needles at the tip, is cut from a branch of a 1 to 3 year old white pine sapling. The lower end is then cut into a wedge about 2 cm long (fig. 9-1, 9-2), with one side thicker than the other. The depth of the cleft cut into the side of the stock should be one third to one half the length of its circumference (fig. 9-3). The scion is then inserted into the cleft so that the cambian layers fit properly. The exposed cut surface of both the scion and the stock are then bound with plastic sheeting (fig. 9-4, 5, 6). When they have fused into a single plant, cut off the branches of the stock in winter.

(b) Bud grafting: If an extremely graceful tree of an inferior variety is obtained in the open country or in the garden, it can be used as stock for the grafting of quality buds, so that colourful flowers or plump fruits will grow on it. This method can be used, for example, for the grafting of the Ningxia *Lycium chinense*, which has large fruits, onto an ordinary *Lycium chinense* obtained in the open, or for grafting a year-round flowering pomegranate with a long flowering period and many fruits onto the common pomegranate.

Grafting should be carried out before the new buds become woody. The method is similar to cleft grafting except that a bud graft should be made on each young branch of the stock. These are then bound with cord or plastic tape and the scions are covered with plastic bags to reduce the evaporation of moisture from the leaves. The cuts will heal quickly. Bud-grafted *Lycium chinense* will flower and bear fruit the same year (fig. 10).

(c) Inarching: This method is practiced for the propagation of rare species or those unlikely to survive other grafting methods. Figure 11 shows the stock covered with plastic. The scion is selected from a quality tree. Pare off some of the wood of both the scion and stock to a depth of about one third to one half of the woody part. The length of the gash should be about 4 times the length of the diameter of the scion. The two plants are then bound together with plastic, care being taken that the cambian layers fit exacty. After about one month the wound will heal. Once the two of them have grown together, the scion is severed from its original roots and the stock is removed above the graft union. The best time for this method is before the trees bud.

(3) Air layering: This method is more reliable for trees which look graceful and meet the requirements of penjing but which will not grow when propagated by cutting. Strip the bark to a width about 3 times the diameter of the branch below the section to be used (fig. 12-1). Wrap the wound with mud and cover the mud with moss (fig. 12-2). Cover the whole area with plastic sheeting (fig. 12-3, 4). Sprinkle with water every few days to keep the moss and mud moist. After roots develop, cut the branch from its parent stock and transplant. The best time for using this method is during the trees' vigorous growing period. Even trees with branches as thick as an arm will succeed with this method.

(4) Bud grafting Japanese white pine: A mature Japanese black pine or masson pine stock grafted with a number of Japanese white pine buds will develop into a graceful Japanese white pine in 2 to 3

Fig. 15

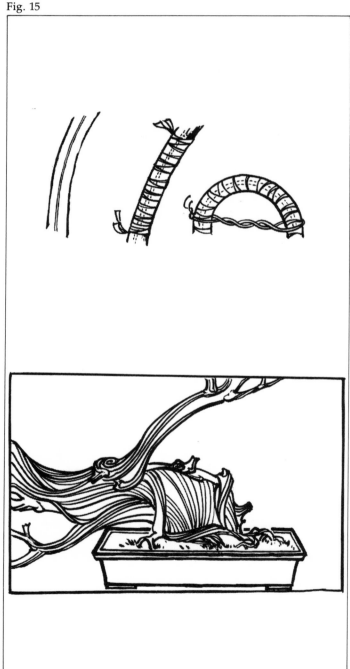

Fig. 16

years, with an elegant, ancient looking trunk more graceful than is usually found in the white pine. The way to do this is to select healthy 1 to 2 cm long Japanese white pine buds which are just on the point of turning green. Because of their tenderness, the buds should be cut carefully with a knife instead of being pared. Cleft graft the buds onto the appropriate positions on the Japanese black pine or masson pine branches, (fig. 13-1), which should neither be too slender, nor too old and scaly. Branches 6 to 7 years are the best. Each branch, depending on its length, is grafted with 2 to 3 buds or even more. They should not be too far away from the main trunk, the first being about 3 cm. long. After grafting, the joints should be bound with plastic sheeting or hemp fibre (fig. 13-2, 3). In one month the buds will gradually turn green and develop needles. The following year, further grafts can be made on parts where the first attempt failed. This will round out the tree's appearance. If the Japanese black pine branch is too slender and too short, graft the Japanese white pine bud directly onto the tip of the Japanese black pine.

If the upper and lower branches are too far apart and an additional branch in between is desirable but the main trunk is too old to accept a white pine graft, first graft a Japanese black pine bud onto the position where the new branch is to be attached. The next year, after the Japanese black pine branch has grown, graft a Japanese white pine bud onto it. In this way you can reach your goal. If the scales on the trunk are fairly thin, remove the scales and graft a robust Japanese white pine bud directly onto the wound.

Post-graft care is simple and easy. The crown should be sprayed with water frequently if the weather is dry. When the Japanese white pine buds sprout, the branches of the stock should be pruned

Fig. 17

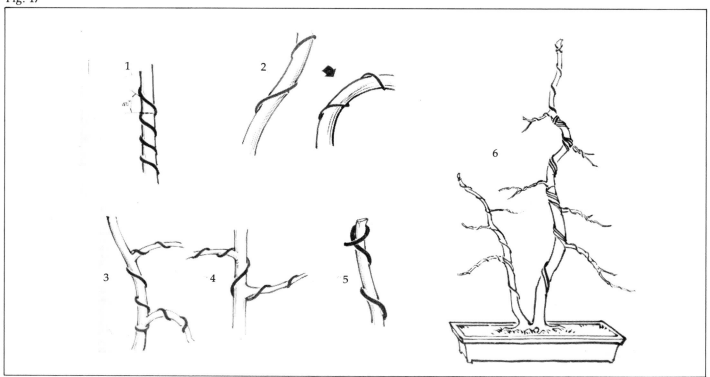

Fig. 18 shows branches need cutting off when shaping.

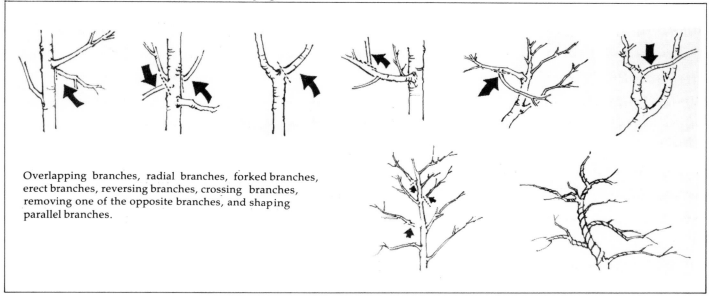

Overlapping branches, radial branches, forked branches, erect branches, reversing branches, crossing branches, removing one of the opposite branches, and shaping parallel branches.

Fig. 19

to stimulate the growth of the tree. A second pruning should be made after the beginning of winter. Remove all branches except those needed for a second grafting the following year. When the buds grow, loosen the bindings to ensure that growth is not restricted.

## (B) THE BASIC TREE SHAPES FOR PENJING

Miniature trees are tiny equivalents of their counterparts growing in nature. Since trees in their natural state have a myriad of shapes, those representing them in the tray should also appear as varied as possible. Miniature trees generally have the following forms:

A straight trunk (fig. 14-1): the trunk towers straight upward, with branches and foliage distributed in neat order. A slanted trunk (fig. 14-2): the trunk leans as over water with branches and leaves in easy balance. A double trunk (fig. 14-3): one tree with two trunks or two trees of the same variety grown in the same tray, one being taller than the other or one towering and the other reclining. The form of the trees may be as varied a possible. Two trees, one far outmatching the other in size, are known as "grandfather-and-grandson". A recumbent trunk (fig. 14-4): the trunk of the tree lies parallel to the tray as if struck by lightning, but branches and leaves still grow vigorously. An overhanging trunk: the trunk hangs down out of the tray as if over a precipice or out of a rock crevice. These are mostly pines or wisteria. If the tips of the branches reach beyond the tray base, the shape is known a wholly overhanging (fig. 14-5); if not, it is semi-overhanging (fig. 14-6). A crooked trunk (fig. 14-7): the trunk tends to lean forward, with branches and leaves distributed evenly on either side. A tree with many trunks (fig. 14-8): the trunks may be of varying heights

and located at random. The grove (fig. 14-9): a number of trees planted in the same tray forming a grove. Trees with stones (fig. 14-10): trees growing astride stones or from cracks in rocks. A withered trunk (fig. 14-11): the trunk is withered but the tree grows vigorously with flourishing branches and leaves. A connected root (fig. 14-12): a tree with many trunks connected by an exposed taproot.

## (C) THE MAKING OF PENJING

When shaping a penjing tree, we must carefully consider the form of the trunk and the distribution of branches, making full use of the inherent qualities of the plant. Traditionally, the shaping was done using palm fibre to bind the branches. Although this method is not easy, it is still used in Suzhou, Yangzhou and Chengdu. In the Shanghai area, however, most horticulturalists use pliable wire which is easier.

The usual practice is to shape the trunk first, then the main branches and finally the small branches. When it is ready, the tree is moved from its rough pottery pot to a fine red clay pot or a glazed porcelain pot.

### 1. *The shaping of trunks.*

Before bending a thick trunk, attach a strip of hemp fibre to one side and then bind it around with fibre to strengthen it and prevent it from splitting when bent. If the trunk is too thick to bend, cut a groove in it with a small chisel up to a maximum depth of two thirds of the woody part and then bind it with hemp fibre (see fig. 15-(1)(2) ). The groove must lie along the side of the bend and not on its outer or inner sides. Otherwise the groove will part when bent. After

Fig. 20

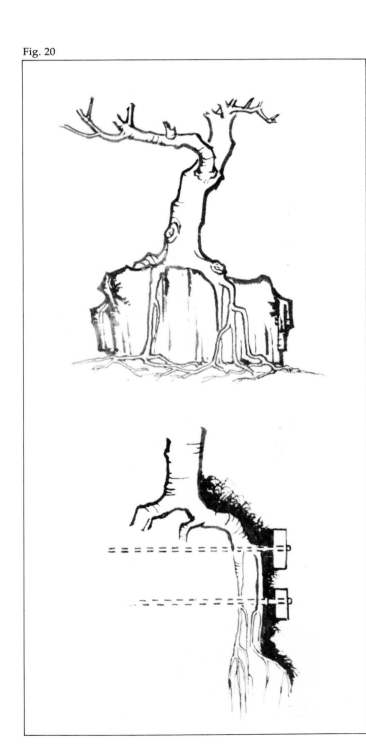

bending, bind the trunk with wire (see fig. 15-(3)). The incision will heal in two months and it does not affect the survival of the tree.

To make a tree look old and distinctive, it is possible to strip off a piece of bark or to carve the wood into a shape. Designs may also be carved on the scars where branches were cut (see fig. 16).

If the tree is very slender and does not look at all like an ancient tree, place an old dead trunk carefully in front of it. The branches and leaves of the tree will look as if they are growing out from the old crunk. This method is hard to detect if the job is skillfully done.

### 2. *The shaping of branches.*

Branches can be bent into the desired shapes with the help of copper or iron wire. The gauge of the wire must be suitable for the branch it binds. If it is too thick, the branch will break. If it is too fine, the branch will straighten again.

When binding, first coil the wire tightly round the branch. The coils should be appropriate spaced at a 45° angle with the branch (see fig. 17-(1)). The branch can then be bent in the direction of coils (see fig. 17-(2)). It is possible to bend two branches with one wire (see fig. 17-(3)(4)). The tip of the branch should be tied as in figure 17-(5). For the tree after shaping, then see fig. 17-(6).

Trees with thick bark such as maple and pomegranate must be wrapped with hemp fibre or the wire must be wrapped with paper before binding.

During shaping, parallel, crossing, overlapping, reversing, radial, forked and erect branches should be clipped off or shortened (see fig. 18).

### 3. The shaping of roots.

To make a tree's thick roots look old and distinctive, they can be raised to show above the soil of the pot or raised and twisted into a coil, much as the thick roots of old trees growing in the natural world are often exposed and curl up like a dragon's paws.

Saplings planted in deep pots may be raised slightly every year to expose their thick roots on the surface. Another method is to twist the roots as the plant grows. (Figure 19-(1) shows the twisted taproots of a sapling. Figure 19-(2) shows the tree with its twisted roots mounted in a pot.)

It takes four or five years for a thick trunk to fix its shape after bending. The wire should not be untied within this period. A thin branch can be untied a year after binding, and a thick one, after two or three years. If the branches straighten again after the wire has been removed, they must be bound once more. But do not leave the wire on the branches for too long a period, for as the tree grows, it will cut into the bark and even into the sieve tubes which transfer nutrition under the bark. The branch would thus die. If the wire has already cut into the bark, it must not be removed in summer as the branch will die from the loss of a large quantity of resin.

### 4. The shaping of a miniature grove.

A miniature grove is appreciated mainly for the integrated beauty of its trees. Trees with slight trunks and not finely shaped can be planted together in a pot and made into a penjing of high artistic value.

Trees planted in the same pot must be well arranged. Some must play a dominant role and some must be supportive. Some should be to the fore and some to the rear. Being different in size, they

Fig. 21 — (1) (2)

Fig. 21— (3)

Small trees growing on a pine fossil, with lofty peak and a limpid lake.
Length of tray: 80 cm.

Miniature landscape made of Yinde stone lying in water. Length of basin: 100 cm.

Precipitous cliff. Length of tray: 70 cm.

Boats floating on water hemmed in by steep cliffs. Made of axinite. Length of tray: 120 cm.

The cloud-like peaks are made of rocks with transverse grain. Length of tray: 150 cm.

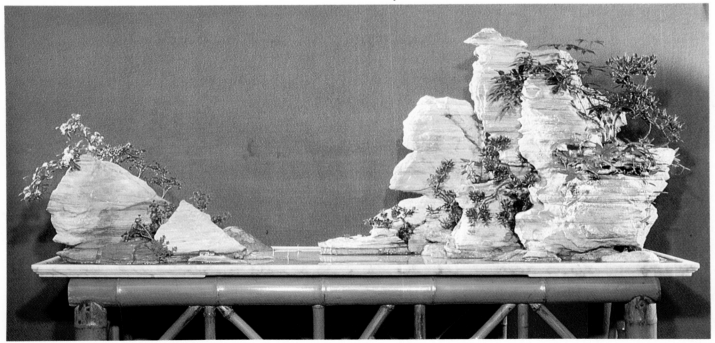

Mountains under snow. Made of axinite. Length of tray: 60 cm.

Made of Guizhou stone and planted with Chinese juniper, the peak
resembles a roaring lion. Length of tray: 75 cm.

Green peaks. Length of tray: 120 cm.

Boating and playing beneath a crag. Length of tray: 90 cm.

Boating beneath a beetling precipice. On the mountain grows a
Chinese juniper. Length of tray: 100 cm.

River flowing through a gorge. Length of tray: 150 cm.

A rural view. Length of tray: 80 cm.

Fig. 22

will form a harmonious whole.

Trees planted in one pot should be uneven in number and should not be planted in a line from the shortest to the tallest. Usually they are divided into either two or three groups. In the case of two groups, one is the main group and the other is the subsidiary. In the case of three groups, one is the main, the second balances it and the third acts a the subsidiary. Of the three groups, two should be planted close together to form a scalene triangle. A miniature grove is an integrated whole, yet each tree has its own characteristics.

Several trees in the same pot should never be planted equidistant from each other. They must be artistically spaced. It is better if the trees are of the same variety. Planting two trees which are quite different in shape but similar in size, for example the Japanese white pine with Chinese junipers, will make the penjing look incongruous. If two trees of different varieties share the same pot, one must be dominant and the other subsidiary. For example, planting a small bamboo under tall pines will make the penjing look more like a natural scene and is quite appropriate.

### 5. *Trees growing from rocks*

This form of penjing may be divided into two main types: those with trees perching on rocks with their taproots hanging down on either side and those with trees growing from rock crevices.

For the first type, the tree is grown in a deep pot to enable the roots to develop fully. It is then removed from the pot and placed on top of a rock so that its taproots hang down on either side while the branch roots are buried in the soil of the pot beneath (fig. 20-(1)). The taproots are fixed with wire and wrapped with moss (fig. 20-(2)). Remove the moss when the tree is established.

Fig. 23   Remove the protruding twigs.

For the second type, the rock crevice is filled with soil into which the tree is planted after removal from its pot (fig. 21-(1) ). Cover the soil with moss to prevent soil loss when watering. Hooks around which wire can be wound to hold the moss in place should be anchored onto the rock with cement (fig. 21-(2) ). It is better if the rock is covered with moss sandwiched between palm fibre. In time the moss will grow out of the palm fibre. (Fig. 21-(3) shows a tree with rock.)

The matching of trees and stones should be such as to enhance the imagery of the composition.

### 6. Trees arranged with stones and other decorations

It is not unusual for a mniature tree to be supplemented with stones, tiny pottery figures and animals, and decorative buildings, so as to achieve a more colourful and poetic touch. Stones should be arranged tastefully around trees. They are better in odd numbers and their shape should depend on the shape of the trees. They should be partly buried in the soil and partly exposed, like rocks in nature. Their size and position in the tray, high or low, close together or far apart, should be as varied as possible, but they should be of the same type and have the same grain. A lot of thought should go into the placing of each piece. If they are not well arranged they will look like a flock of sheep in a panic.

In a traditional Chinese painting, pines, bamboo, plum trees and orchids are often associated with stones. These set off the vigour of the pine, the gracefulness of the bamboo, the purity of the plum and the elegance of the orchid. The stone should be chosen to match the colour and feel of the plant. Fossilized pine, for example, forms a perfect combination with tender green bamboo, and in form, a recumbent stone clinging to the ground sets off the upward thrust of the bamboo.

Sometimes a tree used in a penjing may not be perfect. It may be too straight or too crooked. Stones can cover up such a defect and enhance the design at the same time. If the tree does not form a balanced shape, a few pieces of stone may remedy the blemish. In a penjing with an overhanging tree, a few upright axinites or stalagmites will lend a sense of equilibrium to the general appearance of the picture (fig. 22).

The use of figures and decorative buildings depends on the theme. They should be in the correct scale to accentuate the loftiness of the trees. For example, if a one-inch man is placed beside a tree several feet high, the tree will look like a sky-scraping giant. It is therefore necessary to pay strict attention to the scale of such decorative pieces which, by the way, should be used sparingly.

## (D) HOW TO GROW AND TAKE CARE OF MINIATURE TREES

Growing miniature trees is not an easy job. Only through careful cultivation will a tiny tree grow well and be of artistic value.

### 1. *Watering.*

Rational watering is very important to the growth of miniature trees. However, it is not as simple as it first appears. The technique can be mastered only by careful study and repeated experiment. Usually, the quantity of water required and the number of times watering should take place depends on the variety of the tree, the size and type of the pot and the weather.

Pottery pots are much more porous than red clay pots, which are in turn more porous than glazed porcelain pots. Soil therefore dries out at different speeds according to the type of pot it is in. Furthermore, soil in a small or shallow pot dries out more quickly than soil in a big, deep one. So the number of times each is to be watered is different.

Moisture diffuses more quickly in trees with large, tender leaves than in trees with small, tough leaves, thick cuticular, wax-coated leaves or rough, hairy leaves. So the former needs more water than the latter. For example, wisteria and maple need more water than Japanese white pine.

Usually, plants need less water during their dormant period than in their growth period. In summer, because water in the pots or on the surface of leaves evaporates quickly, more water should be applied. It is the same on dry days.

Generally speaking, on a bright sunny day with a temperature of 10°C-25°C, they should be watered once daily, either at 10 a.m. or at 3 p.m. If the temperature exceed 25°C they should be watered twice daily. The first time before 8 a.m. and the second time after 5 p.m. The first time the soil should be just moistened. The second time, it should be properly watered. When the temperature is above 35°C, the morning watering must be earlier than usual, while the afternoon watering must be delayed. Watering miniature trees with cold water under the scorching mid-day sun will affect the absorptivity of the roots and cause the leaves to wilt. At temperatures below 10°C, trees should be watered every two or three days, a little before or after noon. If the soil is frozen, no water should be added till it is thawed.

In summer, when the soil turns dry, it must be watered until it is well moistened from the top to the bottom. An experienced flower grower can tell the humidity of the soil by flicking the side of the pot. If the soil is dry, it sounds crisp; if the soil is moist, it sounds muffled.

There are two different ways of watering. One is

to pour water into the pot, the other is to sprinkle water on the leaves. Plants like azalea, pine and cypress are used to growing on wet, misty mountains. They are adapted to sprinkling. Deciduous trees should not be sprinkled too often or their branches will grow too fast, destroying the fine shape of the trees and affecting the growth of buds. Water the roots and then sprinkle the leaves.

Plum trees, wisteria and flowering quince require less water during their bud differentation period so as to shorten the twigs and increase the flower buds. Japanese black pine and masson pine also require less water when sprouting new needles. Less water will make the pine needles grow shorter and more beautifully.

If the trees are over-watered and the soil is to wet to retain air, the roots will rot due to lack of oxygen. The tree will die if no effective measures are taken. In this case watering should be stopped and the soil in the pot allowed to dry. Watering should not recommence until the soil is dry. An even better treatment is to remove the tree from the pot, cut off the rotted roots and clip as many leaves and branches as possible. The tree can then be repotted. It will recover after a period of careful nursing under shade. If the roots have completely rotted and the tree has withered from top to base, it is unlikely to survive.

If the soil is too dry because of lack of water, larger numbers of leaves will fall and the tips of branches will wither. The tree can be saved by careful watering and nursing if the period of drought was not too long.

Tiny trees in small pots with little soil should not be exposed to strong summer sunshine during their growing period, or they will die. They must be kept in a sand bed covered with reed screens.

Fig. 24

Fig. 25

*2. Pruning and reshaping.*

To make the mature miniature tree look graceful, pruning and reshaping are necessary. In Yangzhou, Nantong and some other places in China, the nurserymen usually train branches with palm fibre. Shanghai's horticulturalists, however, prefer to prune the branches to make them grow into the desired shape. If the growth cannot be controlled by pruning alone then the branches can be tied with wire.

If a tree is not pruned for a year, its branches will tend to cross each other, overlap or droop. Branches and leaves on its lower part will wither due to lack of sunlight and bad ventilation. The tree will be prone to disease and insect pests.

Rational pruning of the flower and fruit bearing trees will make them bear more flowers and fruits and look more charming.

The method of pruning is different according to the seasons and the type of tree. Trees with branches grown in distinct tiers must have any twigs that stick out clipped off during their budding period. Trees like hedge sageretia, elm, and *Serissa foetida*, should be pruned three to five times yearly as they have a strong ability to put forth shoots. Those with low ability to shoot such as yew podocarpus should be pruned twice yearly. (Fig. 23 shows a tree before and after its protruding twigs have been clipped off.)

New branches of Japanese black pine, Taiwan pine (*Pinus taiwanensis*), masson pine and *Pinus aspera* can grow dozens of centimetres long. If growth is not checked, it will ruin the trees' fine shape. Pick off all the main buds at the tips of the branches (fig. 24). After a fortnight, two or three secondary buds will appear at the points where the main buds grew. These will not grow long and can be thinned later. If the branches still seem too long

the following year, they can be cut short, but the pine needles on them should be kept. Adventitious buds may appear later on the needle bundles near the cuts. These adventitious buds should not be picked off the next year because they are the only new buds on the branches; without them the branches would die. At the same time the buds are removed, the branches should be thinned out. Any protruding branches should be cut off. Old leaves must be picked off so as to let in the sunlight and improve ventilation.

To make the branches of Japanese white pines grow short, strong and horizontally, every year, during their sprouting period, clip off one-third to two-thirds of each of the buds according to the vigour and length of their growth (fig. 25), and also thin out superfluous and protruding branches. Weak buds growing on the lower level of a branch layer may be left. When the particularly strong buds on the top side of the branch layer are picked off, adventitious buds may sprout from the needle bundles.

Buds should be picked off when they are young, not when they have become woody. If they have grown too long, cutting them back may cause all the leaves to fall, leaving a dry branch.

New branches of green maple, Chinese boxes, lovely golden larch (*Pseudolarix amabilis*) and Chinese holly should be shortened, leaving only one or two sections for each. Thus they will grow short and luxuriant.

Flower and fruit bearing trees are pruned according to the characteristics of their flowering and fruiting. The flowering quince, Halls crab apple (*Malus hallinana*) and firethorn, for example, bear their fruit on the shorter branches. The longer, vegetative branches can be shortened leaving only one or two sections. These shortened branches will gradually turn into fruit bearing branches. The fruits of the pomegranate are borne on new shoots from its main branches. Each bears 1-5 flowers; one is the terminal flower, the rest are axillary flowers. Most of the terminal flowers bear fruit, so the new shoots should not be clipped. Plum and winter jasmine must be pruned strongly at the base of their flowering branches after they have bloomed. The new branches will thus grow stronger and bear more flowers. (Fig. 26 shows the winter jasmine before and after pruning.) The new branches with buds on should not be clipped or have their tips picked off.

The tender tips of Chinese juniper and golden cypress (*Sabina chinensis*) branches, protruding out over the crowns, should be nipped a month after sprouting. In this way the crown will grow compact and plump. Scissors should not be used, or the cuts will turn rusty, reducing the artistic value of the penjing. The withered branches beneath the crown must be cut off at the same time. The long branches of *Sabina procumbens* and juniper-cypress must be shortened to the sections bearing buds. The superfluous branches must then be thinned out so as to let in the sunlight and promote new growth. If this is not done, the branches under the crown will wither. A tree with a heavy crown and bare stems is not attractive.

In a miniature grove, the trees must contrast finely with each other in height and in the thickness of their branches and leaves.

Deciduous trees must be carefully pruned in winter after the leaves have fallen. Drooping, weak, erect, crossed and overlapping branches should be cut off or shortened. The length and density of branches should be decided on artistic grounds. After pruning, trees should look neat, and their branches should be well spaced with distinct tiers. Deciduous trees are attractive in summer for their leaves. In winter, when the leaves have fallen, they are still attractive with their intriguing branches and twigs. After years of careful pruning and trimming, elm, hedge sageretia, pomegranate and maple will become more slender, compact and graceful.

Elm trees look fresher, greener and more beautiful during their budding period. Pick off the old leaves to stimulate the sprouting of the new. In this way, fresh growth can be enjoyed three times in the year. Many species of trees become more presentable after their leaves have been thinned.

Branches of trees with strong ability to put forth shoots must be clipped. Their growth will thus be checked and they will grow in perfect proportion. To check the growth of trees with lower shooting capacity such as the Japanese white pine, it is only necessary to pick off their buds. However, after a few years the branches will become untidy and overlap, so it will be necessary to prune them and reshape them using wire (fig. 27).

3. *The prevention and control of plant diseases.*

Penjing trees are usually kept separately and carefully cultivated. They are not very often attacked by disease. But since a wide variety of species are grown in environments to which they are not naturally adapted, a number of diseases can affect them. There are non-infective diseases, which are caused by such things as poor nutrition, bad ventilation, and insufficient or too much sunshine; and infectious diseases, which are caused by pathogenic bacteria, fungi and viruses. Root rot, spot, powdery mildew, rust and black mildew are the most common diseases.

(a) Root rot: Sometimes roots of young trees collected from hills, rot after being transplanted

Fig. 26 — (1) shows a winter jasmine before pruning.

Fig. 26 — (2) shows a winter jasmine after pruning.

Fig. 27 — (1) Before reshaping.

Fig. 27 — (2) After reshaping.

into pots. This is mostly due to fungal infections such a fusarium, pythium, rhizoctonia and sclerotium. Over-watering may also cause root rot, because too much water makes it impossible for the roots to breathe freely. The way to prevent root rot is by careful cultivation including regulating exposure to sunshine, temperature and moisture, improving the soil by applying fertilizers and other mineral elements in order to enhance the plant's disease resistance, and sterilizing the soil by spreading in sunlight, or spraying chemicals such as sulphur, ferrous sulphate, formalin, PCNB-ceresan mixture and chloropicrin. In recent years pasteurization has been used to eliminte the pathogenic microbes in the soil. Using this method, the soil temperature is raised to 82°C by spraying steam into it. In this way, soil nematodes and other insect pests are killed, as well as weed seeds.

(b) Spot diseases: Necroses of various colours and in different shapes can sometimes be found on the leaves, tender branch tips and fruit of both coniferous and broadleaf trees. Most of the these are caused by fungi, some by bacterial infection and some by non-infectious factors. Spot disease include leaf spot, canker and shot hole. Spraying batericide and fungicide like Bordeaux mixture, Phytomycin, Jinggangencin, Actidione, Topsin and MBC will help prevent spot diseases.

(c) Powdery mildew: Powdery mildew is only a threat to angiosperms, especially to their leaves, but not to their roots. In some trees such as red maple, trident maple (*Acer buergerianum*), Chinese wolfberry and crape myrtle (*Lagerstroemia indica*), the fruits, flowers and tender branch tips are also affected. Powdery mildew is caused by the fungi of erysiphales or ascomycetes. Using too much nitrogenous fertilizer or keeping the trees in shady places for too long a period will cause powdery mildew. This disease can be prevented and controlled by spraying sulphur or lime-sulphur of 0.3 to 0.5 degrees Baume.

(d) Rust: This disease is very often seen in cultivated miniature trees, especially the juniper-cypress, pear, common flowering quince and Chinese flowering quince. It causes the leaves and fruit to fall. To prevent it spreading, it is first necessary to eliminate the pathogen that survives through the winter. Trees like pear and juniper-cypress, which are hosts for rust, must not be planted close to each other. Spraying Bordeaux mixture, Zineb, TD-40 or Sodium P-aminobenzene sulphonate will be of some help in checking the spread of rust.

(e) Black mildew: This is caused by the pathogenic capnodiaceae and melialaceae bacteria in ascomycetes. Many trees including elm, yew podocarpus and Chinese holly are subject to this disease. When the disease develops, the leaves and branches are covered with a thick layer of sooty mold, making it difficult for the tree to absorb sunshine and thereby preventing photosynthesis. This detracts from the beauty of the tree. The molds thrive on the secretions of aphids and scale insects which also help to spread them. The prevention of black mildew mainly depends, therefore, on the elimination of aphids and scale insects. Lime-sulphur can be sprayed to kill the pathogen already attached to the plants.

*4. Pest control.*

Antique trees in exotic shapes are priceless. The loss of even a single leaf or branch will disfigure them. Measures taken against pest attack should be timely, effective, safe for both plants and human beings and free of toxic residues and objectionable odours.

Pests harmful to miniature plants can be divided into four categories.

(1) Foliage-feeding insects. Falling into this category are mainly Monema flavescens, Crypto-thelea miniscula, inchworms, Euproctis pseudo-conspersa, Papilio polytes and Galerucella maculicollis.

To combat foliage-feeding insects, constant attention should be given to the leaves. If insect eggs, chewing marks, translucent spots or dots of fresh excrement are discovered, either on the leaves or on the soil, the pests can be eradicated without the application of chemicals provided that the infestation is not serious. In chemical pest control, highly effective insecticides with low toxicity to higher animals are preferred. For example, 25% wettable Sevin powder (1 part of the powder dissolved in 400 parts of water) and 50% wettable Tsumacide powder (1 part of the powder dissolved in 500 parts of water) are effective against a number of foliage-feeding insects as well as against sap-sucking insects. Fifty per cent Phoxim emulsion (1 part of the emulsion mixed with 1,000 parts of water) is good for dealing with Lepidopte-ron larvae, and 90% Dipterex crystals (1 part of the crystals dissolved in 1,000 parts of water) are also highly effective.

(2) Sap-sucking insects. Insects belonging to this category include scale insects, aphids, stink-bugs and red spiders. There are many species of scale insects and few miniature plants are immune to their attack. Their damage not only retards plant growth but also causes black mildew which, if serious, often leads to the death of the affected plant. Some of the species lay eggs three to four times a year but most produce offspring only once a year. Systemic poisons such as Sumithion (1 part of the chemical mixed with 800 parts of water), Rogor (1 part of Rogor mixed with 2,500 parts of water) and a mixture of equal parts of Sumithion, Rogor and Baytex (1 part of the mixture dissolved in 1,000 parts of water) are effective against scale insects, especially when applied while the young insects are still present. Imidan, although effective, has a strong and unpleasant smell. Aphids affect plants in spring and autumn, causing curling of young branches and leaves. Elm aphids also produce purplish red or green galls of various sizes on the trees which not only stunt their growth but are unsightly. The insecticides used in dealing with scale insects are also effective in controlling aphids. Rogor must, however, be used with care because it may harm plum, elm and peach trees. In dealing with aphids alone, 1/1,000 Derris extract solution or 1/50-60 nicotine and lime solution is preferable. These can also be used to combat shield-bugs, which are harmful to azaleas and roses, as well as red spiders, which attack pines, cypresses and roses. When red spider infestation is heavy, use 50% Trithion emulsion (1 part of the emulsion mixed with 3,000 parts of water), or add 3 parts of Tedion to the solution if protection is required for prolonged periods.

(3) Boring insects. These are mainly longicorns, Agrilus, carpenter moths and Dioryctria splendidella which are injurious to pines, plums, peaches, Chinese flowering crabapples, winter-sweets, pears and apples. Boring insects cause retardation of plant growth and wilting of leaves. Serious infestation results in loss of branches or even death of the whole plant. Longicorns or Agrilus must be destroyed when they hatch from the eggs or during their mating season. Dead and withered branches should be removed. Alternatively, Baytex or Rogor solution (1 part of the solu-

tion mixed with 5-10 parts of water) can be dripped into the holes made by the pests, and applied to the roots or any injured parts.

(4) Soil-inhabiting pests. This category includes slugs, snails, Planobis, oncomelania and pill-bugs, etc. which live and propagate in the soil. Some of them pollute the plants with their secretions, others destroy the young leaves, trunk or roots. When such pests are detected the eggs in the soil must be destroyed. An infusion prepared with 1 part tea-seed cake (made from tea-seed husks after the oil has been pressed out) and 10 parts water is effective. Lime nitrogen will kill moluscs and Sevin or Tsumacide (1 part of 25% wettable Sevin or Tsumacide powder mixed with 100 parts of water) sprayed over the soil, container bottoms and supports will kill or expel pill bugs.

### 5. *Application of fertilizers.*

There is very little soil in miniature gardens and the nutrients in it are limited. Therefore, fertilizers must be applied frequently, as lack of adequate nutrients cause chlorosis of the leaves, weakening of the branches and thinning of the flowers and fruit. On the other hand, excessive application of fertilizers will result in overgrowth and thus spoil the trees' appearance. Fertilizers must, therefore, be used with care. It is necessary to acquire a good understanding of the requirements of the plants grown, the sort of nutrients they need and how much and when they need them. It is also necessary to understand the nature and composition of the fertilizers used. Then it is possible to use the fertilizers to their best advantage.

Plants need the three major nutrients — nitrogen, phosphorus and potassium. Micro-nutrients or trace elements such as calcium, magnesium, sulphur, iron, manganese, zinc, boron, copper, molybdenum are also needed but in very small quantities. Nitrogen helps the plant grow. Phosphorus helps produce fully developed flowers in characteristic colours, enables the fruit to ripen early and contributes to root development and the plant's resistance to cold and drought. Potassium helps strengthen the trunk and branches, raises the plant's resistance to pest damage an enables the fruit to grow bigger.

The major food required by foliage plants such as Japanese white pines, Chinese junipers, Chinese boxes and Nepal ivy (*Hedera nepalenses*) is nitrogen supplemented with phosphorus and potassium. Flowering plants such as wisterias, firethorns, Chinese flowering crabapples, pomegranates and nandinas need more phosophorus and potassium in addition to nitrogen.

For miniature plants, organic fertilizers are preferable to inorganic ones. Most of the inorganic fertilizers available consist of a substance which provides only one of the nutrients. However, they can be used as top dressing for their quick action. Calcium superphosphate, for instance, is good for flowering plants. The most common organic fertilizers in use are beancake and rapeseed cake (made from rapeseed husks after the oil has been pressed out) which are rich in nitrogen, chicken droppings and bone meal which abound in phosphorus, and plant ash which is a rich source of potassium.

Before potting or repotting, apply some fermented beancake and bone meal to the soil. These will decompose gradually and thus provide nutrients for the plant. During the growing period, particularly when the plant is putting forth new leaves, flowering and bearing fruit, quick-acting fertilizers should be applied. Generally, flowering plants need to be fertilized once a week.

For foliage trees like pines and cypresses, 3-4 times a year is enough. During summer, when the plant stops growing, the application of fertilizers should be discontinued until autumn. Care should be taken not to apply fertilizer too late in autumn, for this may result in overgrowth of the plant and make its young autumn shoots a victim of frost.

What fertilizer and how much of it a particular plant needs is determined by chemical analysis of the soil in which it grows. If soil analysis is not available, the appearance of the plant can also serve as a guide.

Liquid fertilizer is applied only when the soil is fairly dry, so it is easily taken up by the plant. If applied when the soil is too wet, it may be lost by leaching or rot the root. The concentration of the fertilizer used, particularly for plants which are developing new roots, must be low or it will cause dehydration of the root and eventually lead to wilting of the leaves of even death of the plant. However, plants during their dormant periods tolerate a higher concentration than during their growing periods. Organic fertilizers must be fermented before use. Apart from liquid fertilizer dressings, it is advisable to work a few small balls made of a mixture of fermented beancake and bone meal into the soil around the container once a week. This will benefit the plant as they decompose.

Shortages of trace elements result in unhealthy growth. Iron deficiency, for instance, causes yellowing of the leaves and retards camellias and azaleas grown in calcareous soils. Control is achieved by adding a mixture of ferrous sulphate and fermented beancake to the soil, or spraying ferrous sulphate alone on the soil or over the leaves.

### 6. Repotting.

After being in a container for a few years, the soil will be depleted and the plant will become pot-bound, leaving no space for new roots and hampering the plant's power to absorb water. As a result, the leaves will become yellow, branches will become weak and growth will deteriorate. For these reasons, repotting and the cutting of old roots are necessary at regular intervals.

The time for repotting is determined by the kind of plant grown and the size of its container. In general, this ranges from 3-5 years for plants grown in large size containers and 2-3 years for those grown in small and medium size ones. However, the interval can be longer if the plants are doing well.

Repotting is generally done when the plant is in a state of inactivity or slow growth. The best time is when the dormant period is drawing to a close. In cold areas, the time of repotting is very important. The plant will be damaged by the cold if it is done too early in the spring, and its new roots will suffer if it is done too late. For deciduous, broadleaf trees, the work is usually done in the rainy season. It can, however, be done in other seasons if proper measures are adopted. The plants need to be nursed for a time in a greenhouse if repotted in winter, and in the shade if repotted in summer.

Soils which are fertile and permeable to air and water are well suited for miniature plants. Loams are ideal for their well proportioned clay and sand content, fertility, and permeability to air and water. Organic matter is a source of various plant nutrients and is therefore one of the criteria for soil fertility. Compost of decayed leaves and animal manure, fermented farmyard manure and silt are all rich in organic matter. Five parts of medium

Fig. 28

loam mixed with three parts of farmyard manure or compost and two parts of plant ash makes an ideal soil for miniature plants. Silt dried in winter and then mixed with plant ash is also good. Soils for miniature plants should not contain clods or materials of no value.

Humus formed by decayed vegetation can be found in large quantities in wooded regions. Acid, sandy and rich in organic matter, it is a fine soil widely used for growing miniature plants.

Trees vary in their soil requirements. Pines prefer sandy soils while pomegranates are fond of slightly sticky heavy soils. When preparing soils, due attention should be given to each tree's individual needs.

When repotting, remove the plant, together with the soil in which it grows from the container. With the help of a bamboo scraper take away about half of the soil then cut away part of the old root. For pomegranates and azaleas, which abound in root hairs and can revive quickly, more soil can be removed. In Japanese black pines and lovely golden larches, the main root which grows downward develops much faster than the rootlets which grow sidewards. Each year it adds a new layer of roots. After a few years' growth, this will raise the surface of the soil above the rim of its container, making watering difficult. It is, therefore, necessary to cut away some of the layers of old root when repotted. For Chinese boxes, yew podocarpuses and azaleas only some of the lateral rootlets need cutting because their main roots are not so developed. How much of the root should be cut away from a particular plant depends on the development of its root system. If it is well developed quite a lot can be cut away but if less developed leave it as it is.

Before returning the plant to the container, place a piece of plastic gauze and some bits of pottery in the bottom of the container to help drainage and soil aeration. Cover this with coarse grained earth, put the plant back, fill the container with new soil and tamp it down with a wooden pestle. To facilitate watering, the soil surface should be kept below the rim of the container. Since the growth of miniature plants is deliberately restricted, they are generally repotted in their original containers. Bigger containers are required only when the tree crowns are large enough to make them look top-heavy in the original. Plants grown in round or square containers should be planted in the centre. If grown in rectangular or oval containers plants should be placed slightly off centre and a little towards the back so as to avoid any feeling of being cramped. (Fig. 28-(1)-(8): Repotting in its proper order.)

The new soil should be covered with moss after the plant is returned to its container. This helps stop soil erosion and thus prevents the plant from tilting or falling.

*7. Care and upkeep.*

(1) Shading. Shade-loving plants such as *Damnacanthus indicus*, Japanese ardisias, nandinas and azaleas should not be exposed to direct sunlight in summer. Tender, maple leaves are easily scorched under the burning summer sun. Although Japanese white pines like sunlight, their needles will get burned under direct sunlight if the temperature exceeds 36°C. This is because the amount of soil in a small or shallow container is very limited and water evaporates very quickly if the plant is placed in direct sunlight. During the daytime in summer, shade-loving plants and plants grown in small and shallow containers

should, therefore, be shaded from direct sunlight with a bamboo screen or a piece of nylon shade cloth. The shades should be removed in the evening so that the plants can benefit from the night dew.

(2) Precautions against cold. In winter plants· from tropical or subtropical areas are liable to suffer from the cold. These plants should be kept in a greenhouse or in a place where they are sheltered from the wind and exposed to the sun. If the temperature indoors exceeds 20° C. it is necessary to open the windows to cool the room down or the plants will start budding too early and fall victim to a late frost when moved outside.

(3) Weeding. Weeds compete with miniature plants for soil nutrients and are ugly to look at. So, they should be removed. Some short grass should be allowed to grow because it gives added life and interest.

(4) Precautions against typhoons. In places frequently struck by typhoons, due precautions should be taken against damage. Fix the containers onto their supporters with wire and move them to a lower place. If they are too large to move surround them with supports. If a branch is broken by wind, bind it together and it may heal again.

(5) Precautions against snow damage. Remove the accumulated snow from the plant so that its branches will not break under the weight.

Fig. 29   Rocks suited for miniature landscapes.

# III. Rock Penjing

Over the centuries, it has been the common hobby of many scholars and painters to collect strangely shaped rocks. They either keep them as decorative objects or use them to make penjing to capture the pleasure of mountain scenery.

Long ago rock penjing only displayed the natural shape of the collected rocks. The pots and trays used were rather deep with the result that only the tops of the rocks representing the mountain peaks could be seen. The bases were hidden by the pots and trays. As the art developed, pots became shallower so that not only the peaks but also the twisting slopes and the bases of the rocks could be viewed. Later, vegetation was planted and decorative objects were arranged in the pots according to the overall design. The art, thus, gradually matured.

Miniature landscapes now include single peaks, (fig. 30), several peaks, (fig. 31), and precipices (fig. 32).

## (A) ROCK SELECTION

China is rich in rocks that can be used when making rock penjing. At present about thirty kinds of stone are commonly used.

These rocks are generally divided into soft rocks and hard rocks. The former are usually full of holes. They absorb water which enables mosses and plants to grow on them, and they are easy to shape. The latter are difficult for any processing by man but usually have fine natural grains and strange shapes.

### 1. Soft rock.

Common soft rocks include pumice, *shaji* rock and *haimu* rock. Pumice, formed by the lava solidifying after volcanic eruptions, is greyish yellow, greyish white or deep grey in colour, very soft, and extremely light. This is the rock most easy to process. *Shaji* rocks are grey or soil coloured. They are formed by sedimented mud and sandy soil and calcium carbide. This rock is generally harder than pumice. However, the degree of hardness is unevenly spread in any one piece. The part formed by sandy soil is soft while the part that contains calcium carbide is hard. In some cases, hollows like pipes crisscross each other, giving the stone a unique apperance. Others are formed with natural strange-looking peaks and holes. Some simple carving will turn the rocks into highly valuable items. *Haimu* rocks, found in the shallow coastal waters, are formed by deposits of shells and other sea organisms. Though all soft, their texture varies from coarse to fine. The fine ones are easy to shape while the coarse ones are best used for their natural grain patterns. They must be soaked in clean water before any plants can be cultivated on them as they contain salt.

### 2. Hard rocks.

While there are many varieties of hard rock, the most commonly used are limestones, formed by calcium carbide. When these rocks are dipped in acidic water, the surface will erode. Beautiful grains, whirling holes, grooves and ruts will then appear. A number of limestone rocks are particularly prized for penjing. *Taihu* rocks are found on the coast of Taihu Lake in Jiangsu Province, southern China. Their surface is quite smooth, but full of whirling hollows and holes. Like *Taihu* rocks, *Ying* rocks are also named after the place where they are found. They are from Yingde County, Guangdong Province. The grain on the surface is fine and varied. Their natural beauty can be used to represent mountain peaks, mountain chains or reefs and rocks in rivers or seas. *Qi* (strange-looking) rocks

Fig. 30    Single peak.

Fig. 31   Several peaks.

Fig. 32   Precipices.

Fig. 33   Over-crowded.

Fig. 35   Lack of coordination.

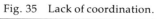

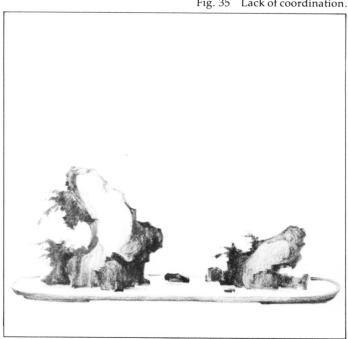

Fig. 34   Too sparse.

are so called because their horizontal grain gives them unique and varied appearance. *Fupi* (axinite) rocks are covered with vertical grains in the shape of wires, stripes and slices. They are used to represent cliffs or huge peaks shooting into the sky. *Lingbi* rocks (found in Lingbi County, Anhui Province) are similar to *Taihu* rocks in appearance but produce a beautiful sound when tapped. Stalactites, found in limestone caves, come in all sizes and shapes. All these rocks are of different shades of grey in colour. The differences between them lies in the varied shapes and grains caused by different degrees of erosion.

Among the hard rocks, there are also stalagmites which are dark grey or purple in colour with some greyish white gravel mixed in them. They are best used to represent sharply-rising mountain peaks. Petrified wood is greyish brown or dark brown in colour. It has both the grain of wood and the hardness of rock. It can be used to represent tall mountain peaks. In fact, rocks suitable for penjing can be found in all mountain, coastal and river areas and any rock with an interesting shape and beautiful grain pattern can be used.

## (B) DESIGN OF ROCK PENJING

Rock penjing attempt to represent the beauty of a mountain landscape on a small scale. To create such an effect, it is necessary to combine various artistic skills with meticulous layout and careful deliberation. Beginners can first copy from masterpieces as people do when learning how to paint. In this way, the traditional rock shaping skills can be learnt as well as the basic knowledge of rock structure and its function in creating miniature landscapes. Eventually, artists must be able to capture the highlights of natural scenery through

their skills in carving, selection, and exaggeration. In this process careful planning is essential. It is important to carefully observe, sketch and master the characteristics of natural mountains and rivers, so that one knows what to strive to achieve and how to achieve it. Miniature rock landscapes, gardens with ponds and rockeries, and landscape paintings are all based on real scenes and have a great deal in common as art forms. Examining landscape paintings, studying the theory of painting and learning gardening techniques will provide the miniature landscapist with useful knowledge and enriched experience. The following points should receive attention when creating rock penjing.

*1. Use the qualities of the rock and plan carefully.*

Design is essential. In painting, people have to conceive the whole painting before picking up the brush. In making miniature landscapes, similar preparation is also necessary. Things like the theme of the landscape to be made, the kind of rocks to be used, and the techniques to be adopted must be decided upon beforehand. The possibilities are limited by the rocks available, so the planning must carefully consider this aspect and themes should be decided according to the characteristics of specific rocks. If this is done well, final success is already assured. The design procedure should be: first design the outline of the miniature landscape, then the specific aspects. Work from the general to the particular and from the rough work to the details. Only after everything is carefully arranged, can the actual work begin.

*2. Subordinate aspects of the design.*

In terms of layout, the main features should dominate and the secondary aspects should play a supporting role. For example, in a presentation of a mountain chain, the rock forming the peak must be placed in a commanding position and must surpass others in size. The simplest layout will have a large main peak in the foreground enhanced by a small peak in the background.

Rocks may look static, but plants make them lively. Precipitous mountains covered by a dense forest when displayed in a tray will give people the impression of looking at natural mountain scenery. Therefore, plants, flowers and mosses should be cultivated on rocks to achieve a more artistic effect. However, if vegetation covers most of the rock and obscures its natural appearance, it means that the main feature has been eclipsed by the secondary feature of the design. Therefore, when mosses grow too densely, or branches become too long, they should be cut and thinned. Vegetation may be luxuriant, but it should not cover the natural beauty of the rock.

Miniature pavilions and houses can also be placed in the pot to complement the landscape. Care should be taken when positioning them. Do not use too many or too brightly coloured ones or their effect will be the opposite of what was intended.

### 3. *Variation and co-ordination.*

Miniature landscapes should have plenty of variation and should avoid dull repetition. Mountains should rise and fall, trees should be dense in some areas and sparsely scattered in another, slopes should be steep in some places and gentle in others, and coast lines should twist and turn. Variations of scene always result in sharp contrast and liveliness. Nevertheless, variations should be carefully coordinated or the result will be confusion.

Most miniature landscapes are designed with some water areas and adequate space should be kept for the water to enable it to give the impression of being vast. When water is combined with rocks, it looks peaceful, while rocks standing in water look lively. When the two elements, one soft, the other hard, are combined, they will complement each other. Over-crowded pots (fig. 33) and pots with only a few rocks (fig. 34) are poor designs.

The size, height and appearance of the mountains should not be repetitive or symmetrical, looking like pens and candle holders lined together or as neat as staircases. However, the variations must correspond to natural rules. For instance, mountain ranges must look magnificent and cliffs breathtaking, distant mountains should rise and fall, and peaks should be high and steep. Changing the basic facts of nature according to one's own whims will result in a poor presentation. Rocks should be arranged in scalene triangles whether vertically or horizontally. Rocks in the same pot or tray should be of the same type with their colours and grains similar or they will look like a heap of rocks piled up at random. Moreover, rocks should coordinate with and complement each other. If the main rock and the subordinate rocks do not coordinate (fig. 35), the scene will look dull and stiff.

Rocks, which are arranged in such a way that they give people the impression they are moving or about to move, look more attractive. Sheer cliffs are very effective but they should be properly placed or they will appear unsteady and unnatural.

Contrasting factors in a scene should relate to each other. Solidity should be balanced by space and vice versa. For example, on a large area of water there should be boats with white sails and the tops of reefs should show so that the expanse of water does not look empty or too weak. While in the rolling mountains there should be valleys, ravines and caves so that they do not look too overcrowded and the dense areas do not appear too full.

4. *A small scene at close range representing a large scene in the distance.*

"A room does not have to be big to be elegant, flowers need not be many to be fragrant." So long as the techniques used are ingenious and the layout good, a few stones in a tray can produce a boundless, beautiful image. The following are some common techniques in this respect.

(1) Relying on the principle of perspective to extend the field depth. Close or low objects should be big while distant or tall ones small. Close things should be heavy and substantial while distant ones should be light and subtle. Close things need to be clear while distant things become hazy. When these techniques are used, it will not be too difficult to achieve the effect of enlarging the depth of the field and thus make people feel that what they see is real.

In practice these principles mean that bridges, boats, houses and pavilions used in the tray should vary in size according to their location. The outlines and grains of rocks in the foreground should be clear while those in the background can be much simpler and lighter in colour so that the main and subordinate areas are clearly distinguished (fig. 36).

(2) Small things set off the big. In a miniature landscape, the shallower the pot or the tray, the smaller the pavilions and the shorter the trees are, the more mangnificent and dominating the mountains will look. Thus, all the features in a scene must be in strict proportion. If the mountain is three meters high, the trees should be thirty centimeters, the house three centimeters and the human beings should be as tiny as beans. If they are disproportionate to each other, it will be impossible to create the image of giant mountains in a small pot.

(3) Use obscured aspects of the scene to stimulate the imagination. Total exposure of all things in the pot should be strictly avoided. The more the scenery is hidden, the greater the view seems to be. Caves should be full of turnings, rivers should wind, sections of the paths should be obscured and pavilions and houses should be half hidden. The scene should unfold gradually giving people the feeling of looking at a view that goes beyond the horizon. Such scenery will provide people with more food for thought and imagination.

(4) Naming miniature landscapes after well-known scenic spots, places of historic interest, or with well-known phrases by famous poets is particular to China. This could also be done in other countries to help miniature landscapes reflect local characteristics. The space in a pot or a tray is very limited. However, if a suitable name is given, the small work will set people thinking and extend the idea it contains. For example, a pot arranged with sharply-rising mountains and a boat in water, named after the line written by China's great poet Li Bai (701 - 762 A.D.) "a light boat sped by thousands of mountains" will inspire the viewer to feel as if he is looking at the three gorges on the Changjiang (Yangtze) River where a boat, carried by the torrent, is rushing down the river.

## (C) ROCK SHAPING

As the degree of hardness varies, the ways of shaping the rocks vary too. The following are some common techniques.

Fig. 36    The main and subordinate areas are clearly distinguished.

### 1. *Cutting and sawing.*

Be it a hard or soft rock, the bottom must be made flat. Sawing is the best way of processing hard rocks which are difficult to carve. Natural rocks are not perfect and sawing will help bring out their good features and remove any blemishes. Before starting to saw, a careful examination of the rock must be made, and the position of the cuts must be drawn on it. If the rock features are not clear, the rock can be placed in water and the line of the water surface can be considered as the place to cut the rock. By moving the rock up and down in the water and observing the appearance of the rock above the water one can choose the best place to saw, draw a line and then proceed with the sawing.

A power driven emery grinding disc or an abrasive disc can be used to cut hard rocks. If the rock is small, an iron bar may be used with abrasive powder and water. Ordinary steel saws can be used to cut soft rocks. For small and medium-sized rocks, cutting should be done in one go so that the bottom of the rock will be flat. The sawn off pieces should be kept in case the bottom needs adjusting. Large pieces of rock may require several cuts so it is even more important to preserve the cut off pieces to adjust levels. However, the cut off pieces cannot be used as secondary parts of the design. (Fig. 37 shows the cutting of a rock by saw.)

### 2. *Carving and polishing.*

Soft rocks of all kinds can be carved into any shape. The tool most commonly used is a hammer with one end every pointed and the other flat like a chisel. The flat end is for carving gullies and valleys while the pointed end is for drilling caves and holes.

First the mountain peaks, hills, valleys and rivers should be shaped. Then the rough features and finally the fine features should be added. Placing fine details on rough ones will make the scene more attractive. Natural rocks do not have a totally smooth surface, but have grains and markings of various kinds. These natural grains should be used as a guide when cutting.

As the consistency of *shaji* rocks varies, the degree of hardness of each area of the rock should be established first. Then the carving can be done according to the specific requirements of each section. Using too much force to carve soft spots will result in cracks and the breaking off of large pieces. The cutting of delicate spots such as the foot and slope of the mountain should be done gently with upward and inward movements to prevent cracking. (Fig. 38 shows rock carving.)

### 3. *Gluing.*

Having been cut and polished, rocks may still not be perfect and some parts may need gluing.

Furthermore, sometimes when there is no single stone available big enough to make a large landscape, small rocks can be glued together. If the gluing is done properly, all the pieces will look just like one whole piece.

Before gluing, paper should be put in the bottom of the pot under the rock to prevent the pot and rock sticking together. Then the rocks can be arranged in the pot in several positions until the best layout has been decided. Note down each rock's position and glue them together one by one. The rocks must be washed clean before gluing. Both cement and resin glue can be used. However, the former is used more often. Pigment the same colour as the rocks should be mixed with the cement. When gluing *fupi* (axinite) rocks, a small quantity of black ink mixed into the cement will produce glue similar to the rock in colour. If dust from the same type of rock is applied with a brush to the glued joints before the cement dries, the glue marks will be invisible when the cement eventually sets. Cement accidentally left on the rock body should be removed at once, and then the glued rocks should be put in a shady spot to dry.

Cracks and holes should be left when gluing hard rocks as these make good places for growing plants later. The cut edges and corners of some hard rocks are usually sharp and appear unnaturally chopped or carved. If this is the case the harsh edges should be smoothed with an abrasive wheel before gluing. This makes the rocks appear weathered. (Fig. 39 shows rocks being glued together.)

It is not always necessary for several pieces to be glued into one solid piece. If they are left separate, they can be rearranged into different formations to add interest to the scene.

### 4. The use of plants.

If we compare mountains to human bodies, the rocks are the bones; the trees are the clothes; the grass is the hair; the water is the blood; and the pavilions, houses and bridges are the ornaments people wear. They are all indispensable elements of the miniature landscape and they are all closely related. After the rocks, representing mountains, are properly arranged, trees should be planted, mosses should be cultivated and miniature decorations, such as pavilions and houses, should be placed so that everything blends together and each thing sets off the other.

It is, in fact, not difficult to grow mosses on soft rocks. Just cut a thin layer of moss from any place it is growing, perhaps on clay pots or bricks. Mix the moss with water and spread the mixture on the rocks with brush. Then leave the rock in a damp place. New moss will grow very soon.

Ways of planting trees on rocks have already

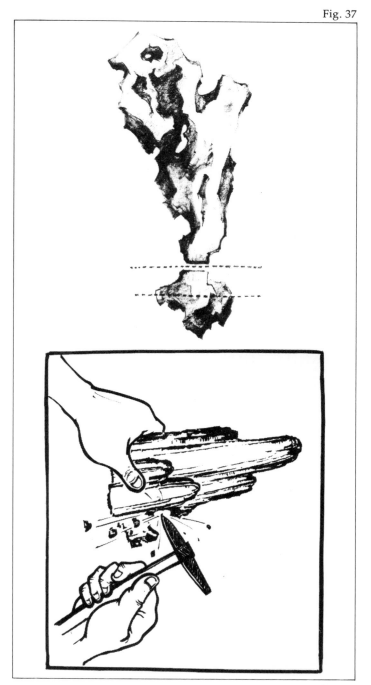

Fig. 37

Fig. 38

been dealt with in Chapter II and need not be repeated here. What needs to be emphasized, however, is the importance of choosing trees of the right shape. Most of the trees growing in rock crevices in the natural environment are twisted and isolated. Their trunks twine and curve and their roots are exposed, whereas trees growing in flat regions are tall and straight. Therefore the shape of the trees chosen must be suited to the place it is to be planted. The most commonly used trees are evergreens. Trees with small leaves, thin branches and small roots such as the penta-needle pine, the small leaved yew podocarpus, the lovely golden larch, and narrow-leaved plants belonging to the red stone-crop (*sedum rubems*) genus. Trees that have already been cultivated in small pots may be removed and planted on rocks since they are already shaped and unlikely to die.

When adding ornamental objects to a scene, place them with thought and care. For example, a cottage may be put on a mountain slope, and bridges may join river banks or dykes. These objects must not be placed at random. Boats, pavilions and bridges arranged in the pot must correspond to the overall theme and coordinate with the surrounding environment. In miniature landscapes reflecting regions south of the Changjiang River, sailing boats should be used, while in those imitating the scenery of Guilin, bamboo rafts are best.

These ornamental objects are, in most cases, made of clay from Foshan, Guangdong Province. There are also some carved out of Qingtian stones and some made of lead (fig. 40 examples of ornaments).

## (D) CULTIVATION OF POTTED MINIATURE LANDSCAPES

Long exposure of potted landscapes with small trees and mosses to sunshine in summer should be avoided. They should be placed in semi-shaded areas where the mosses and trees will stay fresh and green and the young trees will be able to grow. In windy seasons, measures should be taken to prevent the landscapes from falling down. Leaving the landscape exposed to heavy rain storms should also be avoided. In certain areas in winter it is also advisable to keep the potted landscapes in a green house or in rooms facing the sun as frost may damage the plants. If no vegetation is grown on the rocks the landscape must be kept dry so that the rocks will not crack in the cold weather.

Fig. 39 — (1) Before gluing.

Fig. 39 — (2) After gluing.

Fig. 40   Examples of ornaments.

# IV. Pots, Trays, Stands and Methods of Display

Trees or rocks, pots or trays and stands are the basic elements of the art of penjing. Only when delicate trees or rocks are presented in exquisite containers on elegant and graceful stands is the full beauty of the art realized. Moreover, the location, the background and the way in which a work is displayed will also have a direct bearing on the total artistic effect.

## (A) POTS AND TRAYS

On the one hand, pots and trays themselves are valued as objects of art. On the other hand, when they are used as containers for penjing, they also have a practical role as they determine the total space available. When a tree or a group of rocks is placed in a pot or a tray of the right colour and size, they will together take on a new look and their value will increase dramatically.

Pots and trays produced in China are of many shapes, materials and colours. There are pots and trays of fired pottery, glazed pottery, multi-coloured porcelain and some chiseled out of stone. Fired pottery pots and trays only are used to cultivate trees. As porcelain pots do not absorb water or breathe, they are unfit for growing plants. Their colours are also too bright and will clash with the colour of the scenery in the pots. They are sometimes used for cultivating miniature fruit trees or flowers but rarely for plants whose leaves and branches are to be appreciated. The most commonly used pots, therefore, are dark terra-cotta pots and glazed pottery pots from Yixing, Jiangsu Province and also the glazed pottery pots made at Foshan, Guangdong Province. Shallow stone pots or trays are usually used for miniature landscapes.

Dark terra-cotta pots from Yixing are varied in shape and graceful in colour, giving people the impression of being simple and steady. They have a slow but steady water absorbing ability and provide adequate ventilation. As a result, they are excellent for growing plants. Because they possess both practical and artistic value, pots and trays from Yixing have become popular with people interested in penjing both inside and outside China.

As early as the 14th century when China was under the reign of the Ming and Qing Dynasties, there were artisans making dark terra-cotta pots in which to cultivate flowers. Pots of the Ming Dynasty were simple and unadorned. Those of the Qing Dynasty were finer and much more ornate. Calligraphy, paintings and carved patterns gradually began to appear on the surface of these pots. Old pots are highly valued and many lovers of potted landscapes both in China and abroad will not hesitate to pay high prices to obtain them.

Foshan, Guangdond Province, produces delicate pottery pots both glazed and unglazed, many of which are decorated with relief carvings and flower patterns. There are blue, green and variagated glazed pots and trays which make good decorative objects.

Stone pots and trays are produced all over the country. They are mostly made of marble, white marble and white *fanshi*. They are usually used for miniature landscapes. *Yun* basins, also known as *lingzhi* (glossy ganoderma) basins from Guangxi Zhuang Autonomous Region in southern China are naturally shaped in the limestone caves. With twists and folds along their edges, they look extremely natural and beautiful.

Trees and pots must correspond in size, depth,

colour and shape, in order to produce a better artistic effect. If the trees are too small in relation to the pot, the landscape will look too open and too spacious and the trees will appear too young and weak, without any momentum. However, if too big a tree is planted in a small pot, it will appear cramped, top-heavy and unsteady. Furthermore, the tree will not be able to grow well.

Though they vary greatly in shape, pots and trays can be divided into three main categories. The first category consists of circular and square pots. Oval pots, hexagons and those shaped like plum blossoms, etc. come within this category as their length, width and depth are all similar. These pots are suitable for growing trees with straight, leaning or twisting trunks, and trees with more than one trunk. In the second category the pots are usually square or circular in their surface shape, but their depth is always three or more times their width or diameter. Hence, they are called "pipe" pots. They are suitable for overhanging penjing. The third category consists of shallow pots, or to be exact, trays with rectangular or oval shapes. They are suitable for trees with several trunks, fallen trunks, leaning trunks, and large roots, and for groves and trees growing on rocks.

Simple, plain pots are the most desirable. In the case of potted flowers or fruit trees, there should be colour harmony between the pot and the plants growing in it. Dark terra-cotta pots are not as suitable as white, light yellow or sky-blue glazed pots for crape myrtle and nandina which bear red fruit. Pots and trays for miniature landscapes should be of a different colour than the rocks placed in them.

## (B) STANDS

Penjing are usually placed on stands, as this adds to their appreciation. Most stands are made of hard wood such as mahogany, red sandalwood nanmu (phoabe nanmu) and teak. Others are made of mottled bamboo and black bamboo, of which the former is elegant while the latter is simple and natural. It is obvious that each type of wood has its own merits. Some stands are made of natural tree roots which give a unique flavour.

Stands are classified into two main categories. The first category is floor stands which are usually considred as furniture. It includes long tables, latticed stands, semi-circular and circular tables, tall square tables, two-tier stands and tea tables. The second category is stands placed on top of tables. These include those shaped like unrolled book scrolls, square, round, hexagonal, oval and rectangular stands, plus those simple pot supports made of two or few legs.

There are rules and regulations in matching the pots with the stands and each pot must have the right type of stand to support it. For example, pot supports with two or few legs and book scroll stands can support rectangular and oval pots and trays. Tall tree-root stands should carry tall pots while short ones should carry shallow pots. Drum-shaped stands go with circular pots. Square pots should be placed on top of square stands and circular pots on circular stands. "Pipe" pots should be supported by tall stands. In general, the surface of the stands should be slightly larger than the bottom of the pots. When placed in the garden, large penjing can be put on top of stone stools or natural stone stands.

## (C) DISPLAYING PENJING

Methods of display vary according to the requirements of the pot and the position for display. Attention must be paid to ensuring harmony between the penjing and its environment, as well as striving to achieve the best artistic effect.

Penjing must be placed within a small space and close to the observer so that it can be closely examined. Only by displaying them in this way can penjing give the impression that they are towering mountains and ancient trees. When deciding the distance between the observer and the exhibits, it is important to ensure that the observer can enjoy an overall view. In choosing the height of the display, the principle is that the exhibits should be at or slightly below eye-level. However, if it is intended to create the impression of a very tall mountain or tree or immense overhanging cliffs, the pot should be raised above eye-level.

The background for penjing should be plain and simple. The colour of most penjing is usually plain and subtle, and a bright, glossy background would take the eye away from the pot. It is, however, necessary for the background to be different from the pot and its contents. If the background for a miniature tree is a green bush, it will appear as if the penjing and the background have merged. Paintings and calligraphy may be used to set off a penjing, but they can only fill the blank spaces on the wall between the pots and never serve as the background.

Penjing are often placed as decorative objects in traditional style gardens, parks, pavilions, modern public buildings, family drawing rooms, studies and living rooms. Most of the traditional-style gardens, parks and buildings have a neat and well-ordered layout. Penjing displayed in these places must accordingly be arranged in a neat and symmetrical way. For instance, penjing may be placed in pairs on each side of a doorway. They may be placed on top of the long narrow table usually found in big houses, and overhanging cliff landscapes may be arranged on the two tall stands at each end of a long table.

In modern public buildings, penjing must be arranged in ways that match the structure and decorations found there. They are very often arranged asymmetrically. In general, they must be displayed flexibly according to the needs of each specific case, and should not follow a single, hard pattern. The overall effect should be the primary consideration.

In family houses, penjing can be placed on tables, latticed stands, book shelves and window sills in drawing rooms, studies and living rooms. Small and medium-sized penjing are ideal for this setting.

Exhibitions of penjing are often held, as the art is becoming increasingly popular. Attention should be paid not only to the artistic effect of individual exhibits, but also to the overall layout of the exhibition. Exhibits should be put on different levels and with the right degree of density. Important penjing should occupy the prominent positions so that the primary and secondary exhibits can be easily distinguished. If there are only a few exhibits, miniature landscapes and miniature trees can be placed together so that they look lively and varied. When there are many penjing on display, they may be divided into different types and within each type, the presentation of different forms can be tastefully arranged to achieve both regularity and variety.

At present, penjing centres have been established in many places in China and as a direct result of this exhibitions and displays can be held all the time. Therefore, exhibition halls must not only take into account the artistic impact of the exhibits, they must also consider the question of how to make the cultivation and management of their exhibits easier. The exhibition hall at Shanghai Botanical Garden, for example, enjoys adequate sunshine. The roof can be removed in summer, so that plants can grow in natural sunshine, and it can be replaced in winter to keep the hall warm. Thus, miniature trees can grow all year around. Penjing should not be too scattered in a garden. They must fit naturally into the garden to form an organic whole. They should form a part of the garden scene and the two should complement each other. In this way, penjing can play a better artistic role in the garden. Effects such as these are demonstrated by the illustrations in this book, all of which came from the Shanghai Botanical Garden.

Japanese white pine (*Pinus parviflora*). Height: 220 cm. Age: 150 years. This is known as the guest-greeting pine because it looks as if it is bowing. Ancient trees like this are found in such scenic spots as Mount Huangshan and Mount Huashan, but in nature they tower dozens of metres.

Yew podocarpus (*Podocarpus macrohylla*), overhanging type. Height: 105 cm. Growing naturally in China, it is one of the best species cultivated for penjing. Its fruits are flaming red.

*Pinus aspera*, with crooked trunk. Height: 88 cm. The bark splits when the tree grows to over ten years in age. In spite of its peculiar form it continues to grow.

Japanese white pine with leaning trunk. Height: 85 cm. This example is 120 years old. The needles are golden yellow in winter.

Chinese elm. Height: 42 cm. About 100 years old. The stump was collected in the mountain and trained into the shape of an elephant.

Thorny elaegnus (*Elaeagnus pungeana*), with leaning trunk. Height: 72 cm. This puts forth white blossoms in autumn and the fruits ripen in spring. This tree has borne fruit more than 50 times.

Wisteria, with crooked trunk. Length: 90 cm. This plant blossoms profusely in spring.

Golden cypress (*Sabina chinensis*), with straight trunk. Height: 100 cm.

Azalea *(Rhododendron simsii)*, with slanting trunk. Height: 60 cm. Of the 800 species of azalea all over the world more than 600 are found in China. The plant makes an ideal miniature tree, with dense bright flowers.

Japanese white pine, with slanting trunk. Height: 78 cm.

Red maple. Height: 48 cm. The leaves are red all the year round.

Japanese white pine, semi-overhanging. Height: 150 cm. 150 years old.

Speckled-leaved ivy, overhanging. Length: 200 cm. This can grow well without sunlight and is appreciated for its leaves.

Japanese purple maple (*Acer palmatum*), grove type. Height: 47 cm. Ten trees growing on a rock.

Chinese elm, grove type. Height: 58 cm. The old man is dwarfed by the trees.

Golden cypress, overhanging. Length: 72 cm.

Chinese crabapple (*Malus spectabilis*), double trunk. Height: 19 cm.

Halls crabapple (*Malus halliana*), crooked trunk. Height: 110 cm.

Golden cypress, crooked trunk. Height: 98 cm. Age: over 120 years.
This was trained when young to look like an ancient cypress.

Trident maple (*Acer buergerianum*), with stone. Height: 46 cm.

Chinese peashrub (*Caragana sinica*), semi-overhanging. Height: 50 cm. This blossoms in spring, with yellow flowers like birds on wing.

The plum (*mei*) tree (*Prunus mume*), straight trunk. Height: 72 cm. Peculiar to China, it flowers in winter, the blossom having a subtle fragrance.

Yew podocarpus, crooked trunk. Height: 78 cm. The taproot is semi-exposed which adds to its beauty. The tree is a hundred years old.

Flowering quince (*Chaenomeles*), crooked trunk. Height: 94 cm. The flowers are close to the branches.

Chinese elm, withered trunk. Height: 60 cm. The root and trunk are particularly interesting.

*Schefflera octophylla*, overhanging. Length: 63 cm.

Firethorn (*Pyracantha*), crooked trunk. Height: 45 cm. This puts forth white blossoms in spring and bears red fruit in autumn which will not fall throughout the winter. It is easy to cultivate and care for.

Trident maple, with slanting trunk. Height: 47 cm. The trunk is worked on to appear antiquated. In spite of its 40 years it looks like a centenarian.

Miniature penjing on a multiple stand.

Miniature penjing: *Loroptalum chinense* and pomegranate.

*Fortunella hindsii*, double trunk. Height: 35 cm. This is a citrous plant bearing the tiniest fruits of the family. The skin of the fruit is aromatic and edible.

Flowering quince, double trunk. Height: 18 cm. Despite its minute size, this plant is 25 years old.

Firethorn, double trunk. Height: 26 cm.

Hawthorn (*Crataegus pinnatifida*), slanting trunk. Height: 17 cm. This bears red fruits in autumn.

Chinese peashrub, overhanging. Length: 32 cm.

Rockspray cotoneaster (*Cotoneaster microphyllus*), a diminutive potted plant, only 13 cm high, putting forth tiny pink blossoms in spring and bearing red fruits in autumn.

Minute penjing.

A corner of the Shanghai Longhua Penjing Garden.

Peach, grove type. Height: 24 cm. With bright flowers and bearing fruits, this plant takes a long time to grow tall and is suitable for use in penjing.

Japanese purple maple, grove type. height: 28 cm.

Golden larch (*Pseudolarix kaempferi*), wall-hanging. Height: 25 cm.

Yew podocarpus, with sinuous trunk and well-arranged foliage.
Height: 88 cm. Age: 100 years.

Yin Zimin, master miniature rockery craftsman of the Shanghai Botanical Garden with over 50 years' experience.

Japanese black pine (*Pinus thunbergii*), overhanging. Height: 102 cm.

Japanese white pine over 100 years old, with crooked trunk. Height: 85 cm. The trunk was shaped in a single operation which then required many years of care until it became fixed.

*Serissa foetida.* Height: 47 cm. The roots are exposed for the most part.
In summer it is covered with snow-white blossoms.

Chinese juniper (*Sabina chinensis*), overhanging. Length: 90 cm.

*Chamaecyparis pisifera*, straight trunk. Height: 80 cm.

Japanese white pine, overhanging. Length: 64 cm.

Spruce, grove type. Height: 36 cm.

Japanese purple maple with taproots astride rock and branch roots growing in soil. Height: 62 cm.

Japanese purple maple, semi-overhanging. length: 30 cm.

Chinese juniper, with rock. Height of tree: 27 cm.

Gingko (*Ginkgo biloba*), crooked trunk. Height: 46 cm.

Silverleaf cotoneaster (*Cotoneaster pannosa*), slanting trunk. Height: 35 cm.

Tamarisk, double trunk. Height: 94 cm.

Japanese black pine, triple trunk. Height: 20 cm.

Yew podocarpus, crooked trunk. Height: 94 cm.

*Pseudolarix Kaempferi*, grove type, growing on a stalactite in lieu of a tray. Height: 48 cm.

Yew podocarus growing on a stalactite. Height of tree: 25 cm.

Chinese peashrub, crooked trunk. Height: 27 cm.

# V. A list of Species Used in China for Penjing

*Abies fabri*
Faber fir

*Abelia biflora*
Twinflower abelia

*Acer buergerianum* Miq.
Trident maple

*Acer oblongun*
Oblong-leafed maple

*Acer oliverianum*
Oliver maple

*Acer palmatum* Thunb.
Japanese maple

*Acer palmatum* Thunb. *f. atropurpureum*
(Vanh.) Schwer.
Japanese purple maple

*Acorus gramineus* Soland
Grass-leaved sweetflag

*Adina pilulifera*
Adina

*Aglaia odorata*
Chu-lan tree

*Albizzia julibrissin*
Silktree albizzia

*Araucaria cunninghami*
Cunningham araucaria

*Ardisia japonica* (Hornst.) B1.
Japanese ardisia

*Asparagus plumosus*
Asparagus-fern

*Bambusa ventricosa* McClure
Buddha bamboo

*Bambusa multiplex* (Lour.) Raeusch
Var. 'nana' (Roxb.) Keng f.
Fernleaf hedge bamboo

*Beackea frutes*

*Berberis diaphana*
Reddrop berberry

*Berberis thunbergi* DC. f.
atropurpurea (Chanault) Rehd.
Japanese berberry

*Bougainvillea glabra*
Lesser bougainvillea

*Bougainvillea spectabilis*
Brazil bougainvillea

*Buxus sinica* (Rehd. et Wills.) M. Cheng
Japanese box

*Buxus sinica* (Rehd. et Wills.) M. Cheng
var. microphylla M. Cheng
Chinese littleleaf box

*Camellia japonica* L.
Common camellia

*Camellia sasanqua* Thunb. c.v. 'Zaochame'
Sasanqua camellia

*Campsis grandiflora* (Thunb.) Loisel.
ex K. Schum.
Chinese trumpetcreeper

*Caragana sinica* (Buc'hoz.) Rehd.
Chinese peashrub

*Carmona microphylla* (Lam.) Don

*Cassia surattensis*

*Casuarina equisetifolia*
Horsetail beefwood

*Celtis sinensis* Pers.
Harkberry

*Cephalotaxus sinensis* (Rehd. et wills.)
H. L. Li
Chinese plum-yew

*Chaenomeles cathayensis* (Hemsl.) Schneid

*Chaenomeles japonica*
Japanese flowering quince

*Chaenomeles sinensis*
Chinese flowering quince

*Chaenomeles speciosa* (sweet) Nakai fagenaria
Common flowering quince

*Chamaecyparis obtusa*
Hinoki falsecypress

*Chamaescyparis pisifera* (S. et Z.)
Endl. ev. 'Filifera'
Sawara falsecypress

*Chamaescyparis pisifera* (S. et Z.)
Endl. ev. 'Squarrosa'

*Chimonobambusa quadrangularis*
Square bamboo

*Chimonanthus praecox* (L.) Link
Wintersweet

*Citrus reticulata* Blanco var. deliciosa
H.H. Hu
Reticulate orange

*Cotoneaster pannosa* Franch.
Silverleaf cotoneaster

*Crataegus pinnatifida* Bge.
Chinese hawthorn

*Cratoxylum ligustrinum*

*Cryptomeria fortunei* Hooibr.
ex Otto et Dietr.
Cryptomeria

*Cupressus funebris* Endl.
Mourning cypress

*Cycas revoluta* Thunb.
Sago cycas

*Damnacanthus indicus* Gaertn. f.

*Diospyros rhombifolia* Hemsl.
Diamondleaf persimmon

*Diospyros kaki* L. f.
Kaki persimmon

*Diospythia cathayensis*
Chinese persimmon

*Elaeagnus*
Cherry elaeagnus

*Elaeagnus pungens* Thunb.
Thorny elaeagnus

*Erythrophleum fordii*

*Euphorbia mili*
Crown of thorns euphorbia

*Eurya emarginata* Thunb.

*Euonymus bungeana* Maxim

*Euonymus fortunei* (Turcz.) Hand. - Mazz.

*Ficus lacor*

*Ficus microphylla*
Littleleaf fig

*Ficus pumila*
Climbing fig

*Forsythia suspensa*
Weeping forsythia

*Fortunella crassifolia* Swingle
  Meiwa kumquat

*Fortunella hindsu* Swingle Var.
  Chintou Swingle
  Goldenbean Hongkong kumquat

*Gardenia augusta* (Stickm.) Merr.
  Capejasmine

*Ginkgo biloba* L.
  Ginkgo (Maidenhair tree)

*Hedera helix* L. f. argenteo-variegate
  (West.) Schella
  Ivy

*Hedera nepalensis* K. Koch var. sinensis
  (Tobl.) Rehd.
  Nepal ivy

*Ilex cornuta* Lindl. et Paxt.
  Chinese holly

*Ilex crenata* Thunb. f. convexa (Mak.)
  Rehd.
  Japanese holly

*Ilex serrata*
  Finetooth holly

*Jasminum nudiflorum* Lindl.
  Winter jasmine

*Jasminum officinale*
  Common white jasmine

*Juniperus communis* L.
  Common juniper

*Juniperus formosana* Hayata
  Taiwanense juniper

*Juniperus rigida*
Needle juniper

*Lagerstroemia indica* L.
  Common crapemyrtle

*Larix potaninii*
  Chinese larch

*Ligustrum quihoui*
  Purpus privet

*Ligustrum sinense*
  Staunton Chinese privet

*Liquid Ambar formosana* Hance
  Sweetgum

*Liriodendron chinense*
  Chinese tuliptree

*Lonicera japonica* Thunb.
  Japanese honeysuckle

*Loroptalum chinese* (R. Br.) Oliv.

*Lycium chinese* Mill.
  Chinese wolfberry

*Lycopodium cernuum*
Stag-horn clubmoss

*Mahonia fortunei*
  Chinese mahonia

*Malus asiatica*
  Chinese pearleaf crabapple

*Malus halliana* (Voss.) Koehne
  Halls crabapple

*Malus spectabilis* (Ait.) Borhk.
  Chinese flowering crabapple

*Metasequoia glyptostroboides*
  Hu. et Cheng
  Metasequoia

*Millettia reticulata* Benth.
  Leatherleaf millettia

*Morus alba*
White mulberry

*Murraya paniculate* (L.) Jack
Chinabox jasminoran

*Musa basjoo*
Japanese banana

*Myrica rubra*
Strawberry tree

*Nandina domestica* Thunb.

*Olea europaea* L.
Common olive

*Osmanthus fragrans*
Sweet osmanthus

*Osmanthus heterophyllus* (G. Don) P. S. Green
Osmanthus

*Parthenocissus tricuspidata*
(Sieb. et Zucc) Planch
Japanese creeper

*Phyllostachys aurea* A. et C. Riv.
Golden bamboo

*Phyllostachys bambusoides*
var. castilloni
Castillo bamboo

*Phyllostachys bambusoides* S. et Z. f.
tanakae Makino ex tsuboi

*Phyllostachys nigra* (Lodd.) Munro.
Black bamboo

*Picea asperata*
Dragon spruce

*Pinus aramandii*
Armand pine

*Pinus aspera* Mayr.

*Pinus bungeana* Zucc. ex Endl.
Lacebark pine

*Pinus densiflora*
Japanese red pine

*Pinus massoniana*
Masson pine

*Pinus parviflora* Sieb et Zucc.
Japanese white pine

*Pinus tabulaefornis*
China pine

*Pinus taiwanensia* Hayata
Taiwanese pine

*Pinus thunbergii* Parl.
Japanese black pine

*Podocarpus macrophyllus* (Thunb.)
D. Don var. maki Endl.
Shrubby yew podocarpus

*Prunus armeniaca*
Apricot

*Prunus mume* (Sieb) S. et Z. f.
Alphandii (Carr.) Rehd.

*Prunus mume* (Sieb) S. et Z. f.
alba (Carr.) Rehd.
White japanese apricot

*Prunus persica*
Peach

*Prunus persica* (L.) Batsch.
var. densa Mak.

*Prunus triloba* lindl.
Flowering plum

*Pseudolarix amabilis* (Nels.) Rehd.
Lovely goldenpalm

*Punica granatum* L.
   Granada (common pomegranate)

*Punica granatum* L. f. multiplex
   (Sweet) Rehd.

*Punica granatum* L. var. nana (L.) Pers.

*Pyracantha crenulata* (Roxb.) Roem.
   var. Konsuensis
   Kansu firethorn

*Pyrus pyrifolia*
   Sand pear

*Quercus acutissima*
   Sawtooth oak

*Rhamnus glorosa*
   Lakao buckthorn

*Rhapis humilis* Bl.
   Slender ladypalm

*Rhododendron hybridum* Hort.
   Hybrid azalea

*Rhododendron simsii* Planch.
   Indian azalea

*Rosa multiflora*
   Japanese rose

*Rosa roxburghii*
   Roxburgh rose

*Rhodomyrtum tomentosa*
   Downy rosemyrtle

*Sabina chinensis* (L.) Antoine
   Chinese juniper

*Sabina chinensis* (L.) Antoine
   var. Sargentii (Henry) Cheng et L.K. Fu

*Sabina chinensis* (L.) Antoine c.v. 'Aurea'

*Sabina squamata* (Buch.-Ham.) Antoine
   c.v. 'Meyeri'

*Sabina procumbens* (Endl.) Iwata et Kusaka
   Procumbent juniper

*Sageretia theezans* (L.) Brongn.
   Hedge segeretia

*Sasa auricoma* E. G. Camus

*Schoepfia jasminodora*

*Sequoiadendron giganteum*
   Sequoiadendron

*Serissa foetida* L. f. var. pleniflora Nakai

*Stranvaesia davidiana* Dene.
   var. undulata (Dene.) R. et W.
   Low stranvaesia

*Syzygium multifloria buxifolium*

*Tamarix chineris* Lour.
   Chinese tamarisk

*Taxodium ascendens* Brongn.
   Pond baldcypress

*Taxodium distichum* (L.) Rich.
   Common Baldcypress

*Taxus cuspidata* Sieb. et Zucc.
   Japanese yew

*Trachelospermum jasminoides*
   (Lindl.) Lem.
   Confederate-jasmine

*Ulmus parvifolia* Jacq.
   Chinese elm

*Vitex negundo* L. var. cannabifolia
   (S. et Z.) Hand. - Mazz.
   Ngundo chastetree

*Wisteria floribunda*
   Japanese wisteria

*Wisteria sinensis* (Sims) Sweet f. alba
   (Lindl.) R. et W.
   White wisteria

*Wisteria sinensis* (Sims) Sweet
   Wisteria

*Xylosma japonicum*

*Zanthoxylum nitidum*

*Zelkova schneideriana* Hand. - Mazz.
   Schneider zelkova